Telling Stories, Talking Craft

Telling Stories, Talking Craft

Conversations with Contemporary Writers

Edited by
Chris Arnold and Anthony Cook

Sycamore Review
Purdue University
West Lafayette, Indiana
www.sycamorereview.com

Parlor Press
West Lafayette, Indiana
www.parlorpress.com

Sycamore Review, English Department, Purdue University, 500 Oval Drive, West Lafayette, Indiana 47907

Parlor Press LLC, West Lafayette, Indiana 47906

Printed in the United States of America

S A N: 2 5 4 - 8 8 7 9

Library of Congress Cataloging-in-Publication Data

Telling stories, talking craft : conversations with contemporary writers / edited by Chris Feliciano Arnold and Anthony Cook.
p. cm.
Includes bibliographical references and index.
ISBN 978-1-60235-178-3 (pbk.) -- ISBN 978-1-60235-179-0 (adobe ebk.) -- ISBN 978-1-60235-182-0 (epub ebk.)
1. Fiction--Authorship. 2. Fiction--Technique. 3. Novelists, American--20th century--Interviews. 4. Novelists, American--21st century--Interviews. I. Arnold, Chris Feliciano, 1981- II. Cook, Anthony, 1980-
PN3365.T46 2010
808.3--dc22

2010012479

Cover design by Anthony Cook

Printed on acid-free paper.

Sycamore Review is Purdue University's international journal of literature, opinion and the arts.

Parlor Press, LLC is an independent publisher of scholarly and trade titles in print and multimedia formats. This book is available in paperback and ebook formats from Parlor Press on the World Wide Web at http://www.parlorpress.com or through online and brick-and-mortar bookstores. For submission information or to find out about Parlor Press publications, write to Parlor Press, 816 Robinson St., West Lafayette, Indiana 47906, or e-mail editor@parlorpress.com.

Contents

Foreword

Chris Arnold and Anthony Cook

If fiction writing is not just an occupation, but a lifestyle, then this book is more than just writers talking about literature—it's a gathering of artists in conversation about their lives. Perhaps this is the source of the joy and mystery of the interview form: The books have been written, printed, and read, but here are a few more words from the authors, not in their narrative voices, or in the voices of their protagonists, but in their real voices, whatever those might sound like.

We believe the strength of this anthology lies in its diversity of voices. Gathered here are realists and fabulists, short story writers and novelists, Pulitzer Prize winners and debut writers. Their influences range from Dostoyevsky to Stan Lee to the Brothers Grimm. They came to their calling after working as firemen, or Avon sales reps, or soldiers. What they share is an exquisite thoughtfulness about life and literature, and a generosity toward young writers just starting out on this lifelong path.

One common difficulty for young writers is recognizing that fiction has much more in common with bricklaying than daydreaming. For this reason, it makes sense to learn the art through apprenticeship—that medieval idea that a craft is best learned in close proximity to a master. This idea drives the fifteen interviews in this book. Each interview originally appeared in *Sycamore Review*, Purdue University's international journal of literature, opinion and the arts. The premise is simple enough: Take an apprentice writer and put them in the same room as a master. In an era of prepared statements and electronic correspondence, these interviews are unique for their human qualities. Often conducted before a live audience, they have the conversational quality of a friendly chat and the performative feel of improv comedy.

The journal has been conducting this experiment for more than 20 years. The most memorable results are collected here.

The editors would like to thank each of the interviewers and interviewees for being the subjects of these experiments. We'd also like to thank the creative writing faculty at Purdue University, David Blakesley at Parlor Press, the inimitable Michael Martone, *Sycamore Review* staff past and present, and our intern for this project, Lisa Curtin.

Introduction

Half Life

Michael Martone

Answer: What kind of question is that? Blue. I suppose. I was, a long time ago, the editor of my junior high school newspaper, *The Franklin Post*, and it had, as a recurring feature, interviews that were titled "Know the Ninth." Many of the stock questions were interested in establishing a particular ninth grader's favorite this or favorite that.

Answer: *The River of Shadows: Eadweard Muybridge and the Technological Wild West* by Rebecca Solnit, Niall Ferguson's *Ascent of Money*, and *100 Frogs*. This is another kind of question. What is it really asking? It does not, so much, want to literally know what I am reading (I am at this moment, reading this "this" at this moment) but couches reading as a special kind of reading, embedding in the question a qualifier of quality—what are you reading that is *good*, that is helpful to the act of the questioner's writing. There is reading. And there is reading. Our eyes pass over so much every day. We read continuously. But the reading in question, the reading of this question, is a kind of dedicated reading, sequestered reading, reading that excludes the world of reading. The question is seeking a key to a treasure. Read this and you will understand. The question does not see reading as a treasure itself. It is a question that does not really want to know the answer it asked.

Answer: Perhaps. What is this form, the interview? What is the form up to? This form is often all about nostalgia. It exercises nostalgia. It exorcises nostalgia. It is nostalgic for a past moment, the moment before the moment when "Creative Writing" emerged as a field of study at universities. At that time, in that moment, creative writing hitched itself to the dominant critical ideology, the New Criticism, and the workshop cozied up to the methodology of close reading. Creative Writing was (and still is) sympathetic to the critical point-of-view that rejected biographical considerations in critique. The Old Criticism, the biographical criticism that preceded the New one was to be eradicated and replaced. Now, knowing that Keats died young of TB is no longer relevant when reading the sonnets. Knowing that Pound was an anti-Semite, fascist, and/or insane does not aid, in any way, our understanding or enjoyment when reading the poem about faces in a subway station. The focus was now on the thing on the table, and the who who created the thing under this or that circumstance was beside the point. But the kind of attention the interview pays to a life (or the interview's glance that glances off a life) of a writer misses the missing writer. The interview longs for the writer behind the thing on the table, a prurient protest against the severity of the new stringent discipline. The interview looks back to the time when the writer was criticism's focus instead of the writing. The interview is a fossil from another time and is also a fossil record. It records, maybe without knowing it, the decay of agency, authority. The interview is a kind of bifurcated sigh—the rote questions and answers—a longing for the author before the death of the author.

Answer: The interview's drama is unwritten, isn't it? Or it is unspoken. Depending upon the format—recorded or transcripted. It can either be about the slip-up or the slip out. The drama of turning the inside out. Turned inside out. It is an enactment, a public pageant, scripted even when not formally scripted, that invokes, that promises, some minor keyed Freud-lite that mis-speaks, that mis-takes. Or it is adversarial at the same time. A grilling. A duel of wit. I was just watching *Frost/Nixon*, which is an interview and about interviewing and, in the documentary framing of the movie, is framed with more interviews asking the interviewees about the actual interview and the interview in general. The narrative arc of the interview is about getting someone to say something that the someone would rather not say. A confession of confessing then. The discovery (scripted always scripted) that we all are on a script, and, at the same time, the desire (also scripted) to go off script, to truly improvise, to think out loud, to discover in the moment something new. All the time we all secretly long for not new answers to the old questions but expected answers to the anticipated questions. These dialogues often seem to feign originality in the guise of curiosity. And as often the interview does not inform as much as conform. Or not, maybe.

Answer: Or interviews are about a kind of rub-off pedagogy. The questions, yes? A kind of wood plane or, no, more a fine sandpaper, a gritty mild abrasive that flakes off a dust of roughed out, scratched off secrets. The one who answers has answers after all. Knows things. Embodies answers. Or we wouldn't be asking would we? Knows about writing in these cases here, knows about being a writer. The way to learn how to write is this boiled down anti-Socratic method, the interview. The interlocutor not not-knowing actively but, like, really not knowing. And Mr. Tam with the beat and bells and Mr. Bones making no bones about the bones, leaking, in hints and parables, the sought after knowledge on the subject. But this interaction often produces not answers so much as an exhalation of fame, a transpiration of celebrity meant to be inhaled, absorbed, inspirited, literally. "I hung on every word he uttered." The belief, the magical thinking, is that to know one's favorite color (if the one one is asking is a writer one admires or seeks to emulate) will be some kind of ignition, orientation, menu that begins to obtain the sought after estate or position or wisdom of the one asked. This ritual Q&A is a kind of public initiation, a fully predicable inquiry, the belief that the questioner can rewrite his or her very DNA, rewrite his or her writing not by the receipt of new contact but by the recitation alone. Not what is said but the mere saying of it?

Answer: Yellow, really, but blue strikes me as the "safer" color or at least less controversial, comforting in its way, arty even what with the music and all. One does not have the yellows, but the blues. My actual answer to the question about my favorite color was "buff." The name of a paint color I used detailing the military miniatures I painted as a nerdy kid in junior high. I thought I was being clever. I thought I was being slightly naughty, suggesting nakedness. I thought I was being profound answering the question of color with a color not a color. I thought I was being suggestive in another way. Buff, I thought, a bluff.

Answer: Which is easier to write—the questions or the answers? Which is easier to enact the question or the answer? Whose is the interview, anyway, once it is completed? The one who asks the question or the one who answers it? We write (both the questioner and the answerer), that's what we do. And many of us write the conflicting element, the desired desire to appear unselfconscious while we are "doing" it. It is a thing simply done. It seeps out of us. We want writing to come to us, and we want to write naturally, without having to think about it. And yet this form always exposes or seeks to expose the complex elemental periodic table of writing beneath? within? behind? the transparent artifice we concoct. This form is self-consciousness on steroids. Putting you spot on, on the spot, seeking to leech all the mystery from the underlying chemistry. At the same time, the interview protests for and pretends it itself is spontaneous, improvised, unrehearsed. It wants to be buttoned-down as it seeks to be off-the-cuff. We desire in the interview, in both the art and the art about the art this ultimate truth or lie. That as we remember ourselves, we forget everything we thought we knew. We remember to forget. We forget to remember. We know we know nothing, really, and we pretend we know everything we need to know, and, finally, the nothing we know is, really, all we need to know.

MICHAEL MARTONE is the author of *Racing in Place: Collages, Fragments, Postcards, Ruins*, *Double-Wide: Collected Fiction of Michael Martone*, *Michael Martone: Fictions*, and many other works of fiction and creative nonfiction. He is a professor of English and director of the creative writing program at the University of Alabama. He was raised in Fort Wayne, Indiana, attended Butler University and graduated from Indiana University. He also earned an MA from The Writing Seminars of The Johns Hopkins University.

Telling Stories, Talking Craft

WATCHMAKING | DELUSIONS | THE MYTH OF PRODUCTIVITY | CHARLES TYPEWRITERS | BAXTER CHARACTERS AND PLOT | EAVESDROPPING | GUY FICTION | MIDWESTERNERS | REPUTATIONS

Charles Baxter

Watchmaking, Delusions, The Myth of Productivity, Typewriters, Characters and Plot, Eavesdropping, Guy Fiction, Midwesterners, Reputations

Charles Baxter was born in Minneapolis and graduated from Macalester College, in Saint Paul. After completing graduate work in English at the State University of New York at Buffalo, he taught for several years at Wayne State University in Detroit. In 1989, he moved to the Department of English at the University of Michigan—Ann Arbor and its MFA program. He now teaches at the University of Minnesota.

Baxter is the author of four novels, four collections of short stories, three collections of poems, a collection of essays on fiction and is the editor of other works. His works of fiction include *Believers*, *The Feast of Love* (nominated for the National Book Award), *Saul and Patsy*, and *Through the Safety Net*. He lives in Minneapolis.

A lot of people say they knew when they were quite young that they wanted to be writers. When did the notion first come to you?

I first conceived of the idea in high school and wrote—all the time I was in high school—bad stories and poems, which I continued to write through college. But what I thought I wanted to be and would be was a poet, not a fiction writer. I entertained that delusion for six or seven years following my graduation from college. It didn't work out. I wasn't good enough as a poet. My talents, such as they are, were simply elsewhere. They were for characterization, for narrative, and for tracing consequences of actions. I didn't have the particular kind of lyric gift you need, or enough of that gift at least, to be exclusively a writer of poetry. But there was one point in graduate school when I can remember walking across campus—it was a spring day—and I thought "I'm a writer. Whatever else happens to me, I'm a writer. This is what I do." I then spent about eight years—from the time I was twenty-two until the time I was thirty—writing novels that were very bad, which no one would publish. Around 1979 or so, I thought I might have to give it all up because I couldn't sell anything that I was writing, but then things turned around.

When you had that realization walking across campus, were you published or was that recognition something that came from within?

I had had poems published in little magazines and two small press books of poetry, and I was writing for the campus newspaper. I was writing reviews; I was writing poetry; I was writing fiction, and it may have been a delusion, but it was what I thought.

That's interesting, making that switch from poetry to fiction. Did you really just look at your poetry and realize it wasn't good enough, or is this something people were telling you?

Something else happened to me. I lost my way as a poet. I was reading little magazines. I was reading books by people who were getting reputations, and I thought, "I don't like this. If this is poetry, I can't write it, and I don't see why people are calling this poetry because I don't think it's any good." On the other hand, I didn't know what I thought was good, and I couldn't write it myself. There was a way in which I simply didn't know what I wanted to do as a poet. The whole problem of poetry, how you write it and what it is and how to evaluate it, became a horribly difficult problem. I stopped writing poetry for two years while I tried to sort this out. I'm not the only person to whom this has happened. I know a number of fairly reputable, or actually famous poets, I've told this story to, and they all nodded. There is something, often, having to do with being a poet that's very disconcerting. That's not the word I want. "Demoralizing" is not the word either. It's almost as though you have to invent poetry for yourself if you're going to write it and devote your life to it. It takes a tremendous amount of moral and spiritual energy to do that, because there is, in fact, a lot of pretense in poetry—in the world of poetry, not in the thing itself.

Tell us about your work habits.

I have a room over the garage where I write, and I have a desk in front of the window that looks out over the back yard and a stand of trees. I always have to work in front of a window. I can't work facing a wall. I have to work in the morning because that's when my mind is clearest and I'm not a, well, I *am* a puritan, but I don't believe in the puritan ethic. I think that three hours for an artist are enough, if they are three good hours. Three or four at the most. I don't think you have to work eight hour days if you're a writer. After about three hours, I quit. I think the myth of productivity has to be resisted. I think there are too many voices in America telling everybody that they must produce and produce and produce and that production is an index to virtue. I think it would be a very good thing if, in this country, people wrote less, and they wrote more slowly, and they wrote better.

We talked a bit earlier about the deadlines for your new novel and how you were resisting those.

When I was young, I wanted to write fairly quickly and get things out and get a reputation. It was all very foolish and stupid, but it was what I wanted. So, some of my writings I wrote too fast, and I wish I hadn't written them in the way that I did. But now I think I can slow down, and I can do what I want, at the rate I want to do it. I don't have to hurry up to get it out. I'm really taking my time with this new book, trying to do it right. Also, if I get lost in it and I write myself into a corner, I have enough time to write my way out again.

How do you work the revisions? Are you revising as you go?

Actually what I do is when I'm writing, when I work, I keep putting pieces of paper into the typewriter roller, and I'll keep writing the page over and over until I'm satisfied with it, and I can move on to another page. When I finish writing a page, I'll take it out of the roller and then rewrite right on top of it and then go on to whatever the next page is. So that, in fact, I have some pages that I've rewritten four or five times by the time I put them aside. The draft I read from last night is a rough draft, and there are plenty of mistakes in it, which I won't get to until I'm finished with this whole draft of the novel, and I know who everybody is and what they're doing in the book. I don't use a word processor until the very, very last draft. Computers and word processors are not really useful to me. I like to retype, because I can get back into the story just by retyping it. I think you can inhabit a story if you've been away from it by getting it into your fingers, by typing it.

Did you always compose on the typewriter? Did you ever just pick up a pen?

I always wrote poetry longhand, and I've always written fiction on the typewriter except for sections that have been very difficult to do. There are parts of my novel *First Light* that were so hard to write that I'd take the paper out of the roller and write them longhand. There's a fireworks scene in the first chapter of that book and a childbirth scene halfway through that were very difficult to do, and I wrote them both in longhand. Also a scene three-quarters of the way through that book—it's just a small thing where Hugh Welch is standing on Ocean Beach in San Francisco looking at the Pacific and I wrote three or four drafts of that. It's only about two pages, but I spent a couple of weeks on those two pages.

Often, the trouble with typing is getting back into the story the next day or the next week if you've been away from it for a while. You can reread what you've done, and that works, but sometimes, you just have to retype a page or two. You're fooling your mind or your spirit by doing that, but it works. It's like magic, a little white magic to get back inside the story.

I can't imagine that way of working and revising—every page, page by page. What carries you forward?

Well, sometimes I don't do it that way. Particularly in scenes where there is dialogue or some suspense, I won't stop and rewrite. I sometimes think, "If I lose the feeling in this, I'm sunk." I've got to keep the arc of the feeling in the narrative steady, and I can't break that. But generally, it doesn't harm the sort of fiction I do if I stop. My stuff is fairly highly detailed. I tend to spend so much time on the details that I like that feeling of stopping and slowing down. I feel a little bit like a watchmaker.

What drives good fiction? Is it character or is it plot?

For me, it's characters. Characters are there first before the plot. The plot is an outgrowth of what the characters desire or fear. Those human beings have to be on earth first, and then they have to want something or be afraid of something and to move forward toward what they think they want or away from what they think they are afraid of. The consequences of their actions, the chain of cause and effect, is what follows from that, but the people have to be there first. You can write reasonably good fiction with good characters but without much of a plot, but it is impossible to conceive of a plot without characters or people.

Given that, I'm really curious about where these people come from. Do you eavesdrop?

Not as much as I used to. I used to be pretty bad about that. I'd hang around in hotel lobbies, sit over coffee in restaurants. It was really creepy. I think I've finally gotten over that. I've found myself in airport terminals and on airplanes—it always seems to happen that somebody sitting next to me is writing a personal letter, a love letter, and I lean over. It's really slimeball behavior, but I have a streak of vicarious curiosity about other lives. I've really always liked to..."spy" is clearly the wrong word. But, you know, Kafka said in one of his notebooks that his secret talent would have been to be a police spy and sometimes I feel that.

Why do you do it less now than before?

You develop imaginatively. The nice thing about writing fiction is that until you begin to lose your marbles, at least for a period, you can get better at it, and there are certain kinds of proficiencies that come more easily than they used to. It's not hard for me to imagine voices in the night. It's not hard for me to get into different sorts of lives. I was terrified and threatened when I was in my twenties by the idea of getting inside the body and mind of a woman my age or older. Now it's just something I'm perfectly at ease doing, and that's one of the skills, the capacities that becomes easier the older you get. You don't have to eavesdrop anymore because the conversations that you overhear are ones that you could fully imagine for yourself. It's that Henry James quality. You know, he'd overhear a story being started at a dinner party, hear the opening three or four lines, and then he would either think, or sometimes say, "Don't tell me any more. That's all I want to hear. I want to finish it." Your imagination starts to have these slightly imperial tendencies: *Don't bother me. I want to do this by myself.*

Are there any parts of your work that you dislike or that you'd like to see, in future works, become stronger?

I'll tell you something. I think that being a male white writer in America has a certain set of specific problems, and one of the things that I don't do is write what I would call guy fiction. There are a number of writers in America, mostly white males, who write guy fiction. It's about what men do in order to be men, and that's a subject I am profoundly uninterested in. I don't know much about it. I've never gone hunting. I can't fix things. I'm not interested in defining myself as a man against other men. It's just not something I do or am good at, and so I avoid it. I tend to avoid, and this may be a kind of failing in my work, writing male characters who are thinking about who they are as men. I've never been able to write rednecks. I'm not very good at writing working class men, either. I tend to write about middle-class people.

As for those sections of my work that I myself am unhappy with, it's usually because I've done something too fast, or I haven't thought it through, or the feeling in it is untrue—the situation is untrue to the feeling or the feeling is untrue to the situation or the feeling hasn't sustained me all the way through the story. Something has gone dead in it.

How important of a role does place play in your fiction?

Quite a lot. I'm a Midwesterner, and I write Midwestern stories. I think it's true about Midwesterners—unlike, say, Southerners—that they will tell you things about themselves, and they will reveal things about themselves, but very slowly and deliberately. They will not immediately tell you family histories, tell you stories and demonstratively show you who they are. It takes some time for it to come out. The other feature of life here is that because so much of the landscape is flat, there is a quality, I think, of unprotectedness, of vulnerability that I'm interested in. Nor does it have that ideological masculine quality that much western fiction has. At least I don't perceive it that way—which is great luck for me because I couldn't write that kind of fiction. I like characters who are modest and who are struggling to live within the limits of their own lives. I think that's true for many Midwesterners. They are aware of the limits that their lives have set on them. Gatsby had to leave Minnesota and go east to live a life without limits, or what he thought was without limits, and even at the end of that book, Nick Carraway says that he sees that he has written a story about the West, and about Midwesterners. But he hasn't been writing about them the way Midwesterners live in the Midwest. He's writing about them once they make fortunes and rent mansions on Long Island.

Do you consider yourself part of a literary community, then, in the Midwest?

I didn't, once. I just thought, "I'm just a schmoo pecking away at a Remington," but the more you do this, the more it comes to seem as though you are, whether you mean to or not, walking in the steps where others have been before you. In my case, that means walking where Sherwood Anderson has been, Willa Cather has been, or Wright Morris....Evan Connell is a hero to me. I think he's a wonderful writer.

And they were all Midwesterners. This sounds horribly provincial as I say it, and I could make an equal claim that I have learned as much or more from Chekhov or Flaubert or Henry James or Clarice Lispector, but since you asked the question in this way, I would say that that's part of the community. I do have the sense, if you meant the question in another way, that I am part, to some degree, of a group of people who are working on somewhat similar subjects.

Would it be similar subjects or characters that handle things in a similar way? Similar outcomes?

I think it's both, though I don't see anyone around who is writing fiction that looks so much like mine that it makes me excited or nervous. That's good for me and it's good for them. I have close friends in Michigan who are writers and whose work is really very different than mine. Richard Bausch's work is sometimes compared to mine. He and I both get put on some of the same lists. But his work looks different to me from the sort of thing I do. I'm not sure I'm answering the question you asked.

I guess I meant similar in terms of being able to read it and know that it's a Midwestern writer or being able to read it and know that it came from California or wherever.

This sort of thing used to make much more of a difference than it does now. To be in Winesburg, Ohio, around 1910 meant that you were *really* in Winesburg. There was no radio, no television, telegraph service was intermittent. The mail came, but so what? You were still in Winesburg. You were really there, and you were really living the life of that town. Any of us, anywhere now, live lives that are remarkably more homogeneous because of the way information is moved and processed. So it probably means less to live in a specific location now than it used to, but I'm still clinging to the idea that one of the things that fiction is about is the way in which people are different from one another. That's where stories get started. So it's my hope that, in fact, a certain amount of isolation is useful for both people and fictional characters. I like to put people out in the middle of nowhere because it gives their characters a fairly clear contour. I'd rather my own characters don't watch a lot of television because I don't want them to get so processed into the culture that I would have to write a different kind of fiction in order to accommodate them. There is a kind of fiction about people who are like that. Don DeLillo writes beautiful fiction about people who might live anywhere and a great number of the post-modernists write that sort of fiction. I just don't.

That comes closer to fitting in with guy fiction, at least that kind of character.

Well, it's true that DeLillo often writes about power and about conspiracies and about what people are *planning* on doing, and mostly they are male conspiracies.

Joseph McElroy does that, too. Pynchon. You know, most of those writers are men. It's true. They are interested in the kinds of forces that bind people into systems, and I'm more interested in the kinds of forces that separate people so that they become visible as—God help us—as individuals. I don't write systems novels, which is the term that one critic has come up with to talk about new fiction.

You've mentioned a couple times that you are in your forties. Do you see changes in the characters you create that parallel the changes in your own life? I mean, do you wear a seat belt now and, if you do, did you always? How have those kinds of changes come to your characters?

I do wear a seat belt now. I did always except when I was a teenager. But there weren't many seat belts in cars in those days. I mean, hell, they had just invented the automobile. You can't help it. You get interested in people who are living lives that are approximately at the same stage you are in. So a lot of my characters now are living in houses, as opposed to apartments. A lot of them are married. Some of them have children. But there's a long section in the new novel about the main character and his wife before they met. The fact is, though, I like to write about children and old people. I have written fiction about children and old people, and I like writing about them because they tend to say immediately what's on their minds. They have a kind of spontaneity that young adults and mid-life adults tend to lose. Most of the fiction I've been reading in public is about children. I've been reading the story "Snow" and "Gryphon" often...

"Talk Show" is another one, from a very young child's point of view. How do you get in there?

That story was fairly easy to do because my son was approximately the age that that boy is when some similar things happened to us. When my mother-in-law died, Daniel came home from the hospital trailing his microphone and said "How's Grandma? She's not better, she's not worse, she's dead." That line went directly into the story. In *A Relative Stranger,* the new book, there are three little stories. The first one is about two lovers who are in their early twenties. The second one is about two people who have had an affair. They are in their thirties. The last story is about a couple in their late seventies. So I like to move across those boundaries. But I've always liked, and never had any trouble, writing about children. I don't know why. It's just something I discovered that I can do.

Is that because you never lose that self you were? You're still carrying the child with you?

I am. I think most people want to lose that self and don't much care to be reminded that they were children once. In fact, there may be some children in America now who are not really children. I think there are many forces in this country that are busy robbing children of childhood. There are several ways in which I'm still sort of childlike—at least my wife thinks so—so it's not that hard for me to write from that point of view. It's not difficult.

You mentioned a line from your son went into "Talk Show." How do stories come to you? Is it a particular scene you remember or an overheard phrase or what?

You think of situations with people in them, and you think of the way in which there's something wrong in the midst of everything else that is right. So it's like hearing the wrong note coming out of one place in the orchestra and it's the wrong note that you want to trace in the course of the story. That's the disequilibrium, that's what gets the story going. What I keep looking for is the moment in a story when people have been forced together in such a way that some mask falls, either from the people or the situation. I have this idea that all of us when we write are like matchmakers. We think of this character first. Maybe you think of another character to place next to that person, but you put them next to each other so that, at some point, this person can no longer go on being exactly as he or she was, because this person is threatening or doing something to this one and something has to come out of it. Some mask has to fall. This person has to do something that is going to reveal something about himself or herself, which will in turn reveal something about the situation as well, which ideally will tell you about the way people lived at that time, at that place. I really like it when masks fall, and something that had been suppressed emerges. The classic story for me, in this regard, is Joyce's story, "The Dead," but it's not the only kind of model to use. Chekhov's stories are full of this kind of thing. Katherine Anne Porter's stories have it, too. You're not looking for a climax or a resolution. You're looking for what is latent in a situation that wants to get out, that wants to be expressed. That's where the stories come from. You get the feeling of latency in a situation. You start writing about two people together, not because they are going to do something interesting, but because something latent between the two of them is going to come into being. Every situation is a pregnancy. Every situation is going to give birth to something in the course of the story, something that was not there when the story began. There's going to be this third element. It's very mysterious. You can't even talk about it. You can't know what it is when you begin the story, but if the story is going to work, it will be born.

You've referred to the short story as the theatre of impulse. Can you elaborate on that notion?

You can't depend on the history of a character to explain why things are happening in the way they are. For me, among the most beautiful stories are those in which the story begins at the moment you begin reading. If that's going to work, dramatically and formally, it means either that someone is going to make a decision soon after the story begins or that that person is going to begin acting on an impulse that becomes visible soon after the story begins. Frank O'Connor says that impulsive characters who do that are ones who are living more unofficial lives than the kinds of characters who turn up in novels. That's a distinction that's been tirelessly disputed, but I think there may be something to it. It's possible that the reason readers have become interested in the short story again after ten or fifteen years—Cheever, Carver, Grace Paley—is that you don't have to read very far in Carver's stories, for example, to see that his characters are living lives in which they simply can't make any plans. They don't have the money, they don't have the opportunity. Those people are living day-to-day, and it struck a nerve, I think, in a lot of readers who either had lived lives like that or had known people who have. I think it's true that short stories are often about people who can't make plans, who are just managing to survive somehow.

I feel as though these are huge generalizations, and I ought to be arrested for making them.

Well, as long as you're at it, why don't you make a few about the novel then.

Well, I feel so much more an outsider to the novel form than I do to the short story. I feel as though the short story form is a house that I live in, and I really can take you around and show you where all the rooms are. The novel form seems like my father's house or my grandfather's house. I come in to live in there every now and then. I think it's a great form, but I feel like a visitor. It seems so much to me a form co-opted by money and power and prestige that I'm uneasy with it. People get famous writing novels. They make money writing novels. They sell movie rights to novels. They write novels to make reputations. Editors and agents say, "Well, these short stories are nice, but when are you going to write a novel?" It's nice, in some ways, to have the pressure of an audience, but I think a certain number of writers of my generation are slightly, or maybe should be, dubious of the form because of all these things. But there's no other form that's as good at detailing the way in which long chains of dominoes, of cause and effect relationships, trace themselves out. If you want to write about the way in which our lives criss-cross with cultural history or with power relationships in culture, you really need something like a novel form to do it.

Describe your work.

If I really were polite, I would answer, but already I can see those adjectives descending around me like prison bars. It's just that I'm in my forties now and in order to keep going at this, I have to be able to believe that I can start doing something next year or the year after next that I haven't done before. That's where I'm going to get whatever spiritual energy I have to keep at it.

1992

ABOUT THE INTERVIEWERS: **Michael Kiser** was *Sycamore Review*'s editor-in-chief at the time of the interview. **Helene Barker** was the journal's poetry editor.

FAIRY TALES | LITERARY UNDERDOGS | SMALL PRESS PUBLISHING | **KATE** RAPTURE | **BERNHEIMER** REVERSALS OF FORTUNE | CINDERELLA | CLONING YOURSELF | TAKING WOMEN WRITERS SERIOUSLY | BOUNDARIES OF FORM

Kate Bernheimer

Fairy Tales and Rapture, Reversals of Fortune, Literary Underdogs, Small Press Publishing, Cloning Yourself, Cinderella, Taking Women Writers Seriously, Boundaries of form

Kate Bernheimer is the author of two novels, *The Complete Tales of Ketzia Gold* and *The Complete Tales of Merry Gold*. Her first story collection, *Horse, Flower, Bird*, is forthcoming in 2010. It will be illustrated by Rikki Ducornet. She has edited a collection of contemporary fairy tales and two essay collections, *Mirror, Mirror on the Wall: Women Writers Explore Their Favorite Fairy Tales* and *Brothers and Beasts: An Anthology of Men on Fairy Tales*. Her first children's book, *The Girl in The Castle Inside The Museum*, illustrated by Nicoletta Ceccoli, was named a Best Book of 2008 by *Publisher's Weekly*. Her second children's book, *The Lonely Book*, is being illustrated by Chris Sheban. She is Writer in Residence and Associate Professor at the University of Louisiana in Lafayette. She also serves on the Board of FC2, one of the country's oldest independent publishers of innovative fiction.

Until I read "This Rapturous Form," the essay based on your talk at the Museum of Modern Art, I hadn't heard the word "rapture" used to describe a reader's response to fiction. In that essay you note that many people have used exactly that word to express how they feel after reading fairy tales. Do you think that rapture describes the way readers react to any successful work of fiction, or is it particular to fairy tales?

I did notice when I was working on that MoMA talk how often other people used the term rapture about fairy tales, and it was a word that I had also used in trying to explain to people how I felt about them. Rapture implies a miraculous opening up, a terrible, beautiful feeling. I think that it's relevant to the experience of reading fairy tales, not only as a child but also as an adult. Your world collapses into the world of the fairy-tale book. Other books can provide that, but I think fairy tales do it consistently. You can count on fairy tales for such marvelous reading experiences.

These days, fairy tales are geared towards children, and as children we read differently than adults. We don't have to read critically; we can just immerse ourselves in the dream. Do you think rapture is related to the way we read as children?

Fairy tales, early in their inception, were not intended for children. They are now, however, rampantly marketed towards children. The history of that is complex, and scholars have written about it a lot, including Jack Zipes, Maria Tatar, and others. But fairy tales should be available to adults, without being minimized as fanciful or as inappropriate (fairy tales get a bad rap in both directions). That said, children do have a very immediate access to the world of fairy tales. Just like a character in a fairy tale who encounters a talking bear, children are generally not going to ask, "Why is the bear talking?" In a fairy tale, the miraculous and the wonderful are collapsed into the everyday. There is magic in fairy tales, but the magic is not that animals can talk or trees can cry; the magic resides elsewhere in the story. Said otherwise, and with broad strokes, children haven't separated the concept of the imagination from the concept of reality. Commonly accepted notions of what constitutes appropriate adult thought and behavior require the marvelous to be stripped out of us. I don't accept those notions of adulthood.

You mentioned in "This Rapturous Form" that fairy tales, because of their association with children and women, have been "undermined and exploited." In what way have they been undermined, and what responsibility do you have as a writer in the fairy tale tradition to make sure that you're honoring the form?

That's something I think about a lot, and that I work really carefully on as a writer. I think it's twofold. First, fairy tales have been undermined in that they are still widely considered a lesser mode of literature. I know people who've tried to write doctoral dissertations on fairy tales and their relationships to Shakespeare or Auden, and their scholarship is not considered serious enough. That is ridiculous. I think that because of their association with women and children, fairy tales are, generally speaking, marginalized in academia and in literary publishing. Fairy tales are also undermined by their easy exploitation in commercial packages. Fairy tales, with their extreme and appealing images and plots, are easily packaged and sold, and their beautiful tropes are easily appropriated into creepy cliché. As a writer, I'm painstakingly aware of that, not only trying not to exploit them but actively trying to honor them as a widely known but little canonized form of literature. I'm always trying to honor the lesser known stories, and to carefully study them, both historically and as an art form, not just borrow willy-nilly or update them for my own use.

In an interview with your publisher, FC2, you said that you hoped your books would inspire people to take more of an interest in fairly tales. I'm curious what you see as causes of their decline.

One of fairy tales' main themes is the reversal of fortune, not in a rote, capitalist sense, but in the sense that someone loses everything and then is transformed. It's very much a meek-shall-inherit-the-earth world, not so much a hopeful world as a corrected one, and I think we've moved very far from that in our culture. Fairy tales are very humble, but very miraculous. Now we have so many crassly commercial versions, and hundreds of years of fairy tale history are at risk of being lost; I saw a recent television commercial for either napkins or bread that had Red Riding Hood and the wolf sharing a grilled cheese sandwich. I don't get it. This has something to do with Walter Benjamin and "the age of mechanical reproduction." You can turn on the TV and see an ad with a model in a red cape. Everyone knows that's Little Red Riding Hood, but they probably haven't read the beautiful, nineteenth-century versions of it, which are exquisite, poetic, and strange. I think of fairy tales as a literary underdog. There's something humble and beautiful about them that's important to bring to the foreground again, even in the face of all their abuse. I have just as much fun with popular culture as anybody, but it has done a disservice to fairy tales, one of our oldest forms of storytelling. I know there is a very pragmatic point to be made that their continued appropriation in commercial culture helps to preserve fairy tales (Angela Carter makes this argument, sort of, in her introduction to the wonderful *Virago Book of Fairy Tales*) and I would not argue with that. Yet something is lost in translation as fairy tales have gone "to market, to market." On the other hand, I have never met a fairy tale I didn't appreciate in some fashion, even the more repellant versions have something in them for me intellectually.

Both of your books have been published by FC2. Could you speak a little bit about your experience working with them and your decision to go with a small press?

I'm devoted to small press publishing. I've been lucky to have found the old-fashioned writer-editor relationship that you imagine when you romanticize being a writer at a young age, reading about Jo March in her attic, eating apples and getting letters about her stories from editors. FC2's attention to production quality, the respect FC2 and its co-publisher, The University of Alabama Press, show for the writer as a thinker and an artist rather than as somebody who just makes a product that's going to sell X number of units—these are invaluable. FC2 is also an author-run collective. You're part of a whole community of writers, and we support each other through talking about books and reading and such. You're not competing with your fellow writers like you might be at a commercial press, vying for the attention of this editor or that publicist. We're just working together, which is really nice. But I've also worked with commercial publishers, you know, and had a great experience too. My editor at Random House, Anne Schwartz, has been wonderful to work with on the children's book [*The Girl in the Castle Inside the Museum*]. The back and forth on that manuscript was a spectacular experience. She's an editor's editor. For the novels,

FC2 has been perfect. And I chose to publish my second essay collection [*Brothers and Beasts*] with a university press.

You're starting your own press with Fairy Tale Review. *Could you speak a little about what you're doing and what your goals are for this press?*

I've been very interested in the communal nature of fairy tales, so with this new press, I'm trying to find innovative or overlooked works that draw from fairy tales, and that perhaps have been misunderstood. I started Fairy Tale Review Press as a companion project to *Fairy Tale Review*, as I thought I could help in some small way to bring literary fairy tales more to light. The mission of FTRP is to celebrate literary works that draw from fairy tales, whether formally or by motif. We're publishing a 30th anniversary edition of Joy Williams's *The Changeling*, which was originally published in 1978. It went out of print very soon afterwards because scathing reviews basically said this book represents everything that's wrong with avant-garde writing at the time. I think if you read the book as drawing aesthetically and philosophically from fairy tales it becomes undeniable that this is an incredible, miraculous, overlooked American masterpiece, and I want to give it another chance. Joy Williams is a real visionary, an intellectual treasure, and this book was way ahead of its time in some of its darkest feminist, ecological, and literary tropes. Rick Moody has contributed a wonderful foreword, and the book will be published in 2008. This first season, I'm also publishing a poetry collection called Pilot (Johann the Carousel Horse), a terrific book of poetry by Johannes Goransonn, the Swedish-American poet and translator. The book is in Swedish and English, and I'm describing it as a nursery rhyme gone wrong. It's absolutely inventive and new.

How has your role as an editor affected you as a writer? With FTR, *you're obviously helping to advance the form, but do you find it helps your own work by keeping you excited about what's out there, or does the workload hinder your writing?*

I find that editing is very exciting and I am so grateful I have the chance to celebrate the form and talk to others about it. It's very important to me, that part of my work. But if I could clone myself a few times (and maintain complete control of my clones, unless some benevolent and reliable creature could be assigned that particular job, saving me even more time) I would. Wouldn't you?

Maybe you could speak a bit about how fairy tales came about. They started as an oral form, but when were they written down as we know them?

They have a long history of publication beginning with the inception of printing, which historians and scholars have carefully researched and documented. There are some really good books on that subject which trace the evolution of specific stories from oral to literary, and from "free" to "sold": what details were added, what details were excised, what the illustrations were like—and how such publication helps save the stories from extinction, but alters them too. Little Red Riding Hood is a perfect example of this. The earliest known literary version, according to many, is usually called, "The Story of Grandmother." In it, Red Riding Hood, who is just called "a little girl," does a strip tease for the wolf before she gets in bed with him, changes her mind when he says he's going to eat her, and to get away tells him she needs to relieve herself. At first, the wolf wants her to do it in the bed, but she persuades him to let her outside. He ties a rope to her leg, but once outside she ties the rope to a tree and runs home. In the version most of my students now know, the wolf eats grandmother and Little Red, and a huntsman saves them. Then there are versions where no one is eaten at all. There are all these different versions, but the tale of a little girl choosing "the path of needles," stripped naked and saving herself, that one is not canonized. So the shift from oral to literary involved more than just printing and marketing, but motifs and politics of the story—just some of its possibilities as art.

Since this is an oral tradition that at some point got transcribed, maybe there can be no answer to this question, but when you think of "the real version" of fairy tales, what period are you thinking back to?

That's something I love about fairy tales: nobody can say there was an original fairy tale. Jack Zipes often says, "there is no such thing as 'the fairy tale.'" There are earlier and earlier versions that scholars discover, peeling back the layers of history in literature to find, but you could never actually find the first one—or at least, not in my lifetime. Angela Carter's great comment was, "Who first invented meatballs?

In what country? Is there a definitive recipe for potato soup? Think in terms of the domestic arts. 'This is how I make potato soup." As a novelist, I work from specific translations, and those are the ones that I think of as the real versions—for my novels. But as a scholar of fairy tales I just read and read, and I could never know what was the original. The most learned scholars on fairy tales—Maria Tartar, Jack Zipes, Marina Warner—I think they would say they didn't know either. There are people who would make more connections, academically, trace them back to myths, to the Bible, or to oral versions, but they could never definitively say "this is the real Cinderella." There have been many versions of Cinderella for hundreds of years. And I love that, the endlessness of it.

We listed all the fairy tales that we could think of and they're almost exclusively about girls. And one of the reviews of the first issue of Fairy Tale Review *pointed out that female authors in the magazine outnumbered males three-to-one. What can you say about gender and the fairy tale?*

Brothers and Beasts is a collection of essays by twenty-four men writing about their favorite fairy tales. A lot of them wrote about fairy tales that did feature girl characters, but there are more fairy tales with boys in them than you'd know if you had only read the stories Western culture encouraged in the popular canon. But I think that boys haven't been allowed access to fairy tales in the same way and this is related to canonization, and to Andre Breton's argument about children being weaned from the marvelous—boys are weaned more violently from it than girls (and I'd argue that, despite the popularity of boy characters like Harry Potter). The fairy tales that our culture has really celebrated and marketed, Beauty and the Beast, Cinderella, Little Red Riding Hood, Hansel & Gretel, Snow White, these are really girls' adventure stories.

A couple of high-profile writers I approached to write for *Brothers and Beasts* actually declined because they thought that they wouldn't be taken as seriously as writers if they professed an interest for fairy tales. I thought, "What? Are you really saying this?" But the men who did write for the book were so excited to talk about their love of fairy tales. A lot of them said nobody had ever bothered to ask them about it. They also said it made them feel very vulnerable. I respect that. It speaks to the power of the tales on our lives as writers.

When editors are asked, "Why do you have the eight men in this issue and one woman?" or, "Why are eight novels in this week's *New York Times Book Review* by men and one is by a woman?" they always say some version of "Oh, goodness. Gender has nothing to do with it. These are just the best writers to feature." Yeah, right. Clearly, it is much harder for women writers to be taken seriously as intellectuals in this country. Would you ever refer to Jonathan Safran Foer as "a male writer"? I doubt it. It is possible this clear and unjustifiable imbalance has affected me as an editor and I'm inclined to tilt things in favor of women; however, based on your numbers, men apparently have a much easier time getting into the journal, since the submission ratio is probably ten-to-one women to men, and the publication ratio, as you point out, is three-to-one women to men. So now that it's pointed out to me I see that perhaps I am being more hard on the women who submit. That's something I will look at.

You've talked a lot about fairy tales and their particular aesthetics. Could you give us a brief definition of what a fairy tale is, and how they are different from folk tales or magic realism?

Here's where the field of fairy-tale studies is so interesting because there are many different definitions of fairy tales. You could look at somebody like Vladimir Propp, a structuralist, who says, "If a story has the following components, then it is a fairy tale." Others define a fairy tale more broadly as a folk tale that has magic in it. (Zaubmärchen is the German word.) A writer I love on fairy tales, Max Luthi, who is a little controversial for some scholars in fairy-tale studies because he's so aesthetically inclined (to the exclusion of politics) has written expositions on their formal qualities which I treasure as a novelist. I strongly recommend his book *The European Fairy Tale: Form and Function.*

Are your novels fairy tales? In what way are they not fairy tales?

There's an old form of fairy tale from the nineteenth century called the novella fairy tale. I haven't read any, but I still like to think that I'm working in that form while reinventing it. I hope I'm creating a new form of fairy tale, and fairy-tale collection, with my novels.

On a line level, what are some elements that you see as constructing the "feel" of a fairy tale—sentence structure, for instance, or diction?

This would vary from writer to writer. For me, I mean in my novels, I'm interested in a translated quality, in abstraction, in flatness, in reversal, in a metallic feel to the prose. Fixity. An off-quality that also has clarity and music to it.

Your books are marketed as novels, but they certainly push the boundary of what a novel is and can do. They experiment with point of view and time and structure, but the bigger experiment seems to be the way you combine forms—the novel as a long, middle-class, adult form and the fairy tale as a short story for children. How much are you conscious of formal experimentation when you write?

When I write, I try not to be conscious of any of that. I just read an interview with Lynda Barry, who is absolutely wonderful, who described herself as "sort of the world's slowest secretary" when she writes. This is how I feel, too. I am trying incredibly hard to find the words that I need and it takes every available part of my conscious brain to do it. Of course, when I'm not writing, I think about the boundaries of form—or at least, other people's ideas about them. By definition, every novel is new, and therefore an experiment. I also like Randall Jarrell's definition that a novel is "a long prose work that has something wrong with it." I know that my novels are definitely combining forms—the form of the fairy tale, the fairy-tale collection, the bildungsroman, the novel-of-ideas, the illustration. I was influenced early on in my thinking about form as, for each writer, an entity unto itself, an entity I had to find in myself, in language, by Guy Davenport's *Every Force Evolves a Form*, which the poet Jane Miller introduced to me and some lucky others in a class in graduate school.

I'm curious to talk about your books as a series. You've said there are twelve of them that you're thinking about writing. How much of the material did you have planned before you published the first book?

Well, hopefully I'll write twelve, if I live long enough, though the first three also exist as a trio. The first book took many years to write because I felt I was committing to a form that I was going to have to live with for a very long time. I did know that I wanted it to be a roman-fleuve, a river novel—it sounds so much less romantic in English, doesn't it? In any case, it means a series of entwined but stand-alone books. River novels are not necessarily chronological; that is *The Complete Tales of Merry Gold* isn't a sequel to *Ketzia*, even though the back cover calls it a sequel. (Oh well.) It took me a long time to figure out the form for this sequence of novels, because I thought, "I'd better get this right because I'm going to have to write them all like this." I always knew the first three were going to be Ketzia, Merry, and Lucy. The fourth one is going to take place earlier in the 20th century, in Latvia. I have a long list. At one point it was up to forty books long. I made that list in a grubby hotel room in Seattle in 1998, having stayed up all night after a rock show. At that point, I had been working on the first novel for two years already. But I didn't think about the second book while I wrote the first one even though I knew it would be Merry. I lived entirely in Ketzia. My loyalty had to be to her. When I wrote Merry, I wrote her book with fairy tale books and the first novel propped up on my desk, in conversation with them, but my loyalty was entirely with Merry. Now that I'm working on a third novel, my desk is getting a little bit crowded and I'm feeling a little psychotic.

In your first two novels, there are differences in the way Ketzia and Merry remember things, like the "punish" scene with the daddy longlegs. How are we to read those discrepancies, and is it rare in this river novel form to revisit the same event from different perspectives?

I'm not an expert on the form when it comes to other writers' examples, so I'm not sure about that aspect. But the discrepancies are essential in this series. There are going to be discrepancies because I'm exploring different existential realities. What's the real story of what happened to these girls? There isn't a real one. They each have their own way of experiencing and surviving life. There are some details that some readers might regard as inconsistencies, but these differences are there on purpose. Of course, in part I do this as a novelist to comment on the question you asked earlier about the "real version" of a fairy tale. They are all real.

It was interesting moving from one book to the next. I found myself quite impatient with Ketzia while I was writing Merry, and my editor said the same thing. He said, "I'm sort of worried about reading

Merry because I just think I'm going to hate her." But then he read Merry and said, "Gosh, I thought I was going to hate Merry, but now I kind of hate Ketzia." We both started to prefer Merry's version of things. If a reader hates the last protagonist while reading about the next one, maybe that means I've succeeded. [I Laugh]

Although the books were published in the opposite order, you've said that you think people should read Merry first. Why is that?

It's probably a shallow psychological desire. As a writer, whatever book you most recently wrote, some part of you thinks it'd be better than the one you wrote before. Otherwise you're getting worse as a writer, correct? But I know that isn't the case; I'm always as flawed as ever! So I think it has more to do with my sympathies being with Merry at this time. I just had to shift my loyalty to write Merry. My father's reaction to Ketzia was, "Why couldn't she just help herself?" I was mad about that for a couple of years, but now I see what he means. When I finish Lucy, I'll probably think people should read her first, because I'll think "Merry's such a bitch." Really, now that I think about it, in the end I'd like the books to be read in the order I wrote them.

So as you're working on the Lucy book, is your perspective of the characters changing again? How is your experience with Lucy altering your conception of the books?

When I wrote Merry, it was almost like a photograph negative. The whole series is like taping three mirrors together in a triangle. Lucy adds the third panel; you can see the girls from all sides now. I do find that Lucy is changing things. Her sisters were bored by her, really. Merry used her as a partner in crime, and Ketzia distrusted her, but Lucy is fairly shallow, and airy-fairy. Lucy having her own book is complicated because in the first two novels, she's in the background, painting her fingernails, living on the surface of things. But the book can't be shallow just because she is. I've had to turn a cold eye on Merry and Ketzia, which is sad.

Can you talk about the insistent, "I want to tell you something, so listen," that starts the Ketzia book, is echoed later in that book, and is in the Merry book as well? It reminded me of the "Hwæt" at the beginning of Beowulf, in the way it calls for the reader's attention. Are these parts of one long tradition?

It is a traditional invocation in fairy tales, along with the way some of the chapters end, "I've finished my story, I'm going to have a glass of vodka." These are tropes that show up in fairy tales, where the teller says or author writes, in some version of this, "I'm going to tell you something so listen." I needed something like that for these girls in particular. I needed to start with that urgency and then subvert it with the impossibility of them ever saying what happened. Merry's not the real victimizer in this story. They're all suffering at the hands of a nameless victimizer, but it's something they'll never tell.

It's interesting that your novels have illustrations sprinkled into them, like a children's book of fairy tales. Some of the photographs are personal, of you and your sister. By including them, are you consciously toying with meta-fiction?

I am glad you see the books as "like a children's book of fairy tales"—thank you for noticing that! I do so want the books to be some version of a fairy-tale collection, all the books together on the shelf to be like a row of fairy-tale books. So they needed illustrations. Some of the illustrations are of my sister; I won't admit officially that any of them are of me personally. One of the illustrations in Merry, a photograph of sewing labels that are embroidered with the words "Made Especially with You in Mind by Merry Gold," is attributed in the illustration credits with the line "Courtesy of Merry Gold." A copy-editor or proofreader (I can't remember which) who was hired by my publisher had a lot of trouble with that and kept wanting to change it to "Courtesy of Kate Bernheimer." This person, for a long time in the editorial process, kept insisting that it would be illegal to attribute anything in the book to an imaginary character, insisting that this opened us up to a copyright lawsuit if someone came forth and said, "No! I'm the one who ordered those sewing labels and provided them to Kate Bernheimer! Copyright for the sewing labels does not belong to Merry Gold!" Eventually I persuaded my publisher to include the attribution to Merry Gold, something that was deeply important to me. Is this the same thing as "consciously toying with meta-fiction"? It is indeed, though I'll mainly leave that to the critics to discuss. I have to admit that on another level, it just made me happy for poor Merry Gold when I got those sewing labels for her in the mail. It is possible this issue of sewing labels and family photographs reveals me to be a very simple person who is rather easily amused by my own private antics, and not as a great intellectual. (Oh dear.) (Would a "male writer" admit that?)

2008

ABOUT THE INTERVIEWERS: **Jon Sealy** holds an MFA from Purdue University and lives in Richmond, Virginia. His fiction has appeared in *Freight Stories, American Polymath*, and the *South Carolina Review*. At the time of the interview, he was fiction editor at *Sycamore Review*. **Benjamin Kolp** is a graduate of Purdue University's MFA in Creative Writing Program. He was an editorial assistant for the journal at the time of the interview.

SANDBAGGING | THE DIFFERENCE BETWEEN RIGHT AND WRONG | LARRY | BRUTALITY | BROWN | CRAZY PEOPLE | TELLING STORIES | HAPPY ENDINGS

Larry Brown

The Difference Between Right and Wrong, Sandbagging, Brutality, Crazy People, Happy Endings

Larry Brown was born and lived in Oxford, Mississippi. In 1980, he was a captain in the Oxford Fire Department when he began writing in his spare time. He published his first book, a story collection called *Facing the Music*, in 1988. He published his first novel, *Dirty Work*, in 1989, and seven more books, including *On Fire*, a collection of essays, before he died of an apparent heart attack in 2004.

He was the first two-time winner of the Southern Book Award for Fiction, which he won in 1992 for his novel, *Joe*, and again in 1997 for his novel, *Father and Son*. In 1998, he received a Lila Wallace-Readers Digest Award. In 2000, the State of Mississippi granted him a Governor's Award For Excellence in the Arts. For one semester, Brown taught as a writer-in-residence in the creative writing program at the University of Mississippi, temporarily taking over the position held by his friend Barry Hannah. He later served as visiting writer at the University of Montana in Missoula, and taught briefly at other colleges throughout the United States.

Larry Brown is telling a story...

I had some crazy guy showed up one time and he was waiting on me when I got there. I'd been over at my place cutting wood. I was hot, tired, dirty, sweaty and I had my overalls on, they were just soaked solid with sweat. Been running the chainsaw all evening. And he was there in this beat up old car that was just loaded to the top with clothes and stuff. His story was that he had been falsely imprisoned. I started talking to him and he wanted me to write a book or a movie about his life. And that's what some people want. That's one of the reasons I had to get my phone number changed to an unlisted number, because all these people would see me on television or something and they'd call me up and tell me all these wild stories, these horrible stories of persecution. This guy was there, and like I said, my children were there playing basketball. Their momma hadn't come home from work yet. They'd come home from school and were playing basketball in the yard. My mother-in-law lives right across the driveway. So I talked to the guy for a few moments and I noticed he had a damn tape recorder down in his pocket and he was taping what I was saying. And I finally just told him, "Mister, listen: I'm hot, I'm tired, I'm ready to go take me a shower." And that's really the only time that I've really been worried about anybody. You just can't ever tell what you might encounter out there.

You've said that whenever two people get together they start telling each other stories. You're often considered a Southern writer, and many other Southern writers attribute their becoming writers to the Southern storytelling tradition. How does that tradition work in your own writing? How has it affected what you do?

I consider myself a storyteller foremost. Everybody grows up hearing stories passed down from your grandmother, your grandfather, your daddy and all of them. And then if you really start paying attention to people, you find out that they're telling stories all the time. It can be as simple as something that happened yesterday, or something that happened to somebody else. I just take all that stuff I hear and all the stuff I can imagine, my memory and experience of what it is to be alive, and use that to build my stories.

Do you think the storytelling tradition has changed at all?

I don't think so. I was sitting and talking to my son the other night after everybody else had gone to bed. We were just sitting there watching television and talking and I started telling him about something that had happened when I was a little boy. Things I'd never told him before, and he's eighteen years old. He was digging hearing about all of it: "What about this? What about this?" And I'm telling him all about it. We were just sitting there telling stories. And he tells me stories, too, and he tells me some of the funniest stories that I've ever heard. He just cracks me up, all this stuff that he comes home with. All the stuff that's going on with him and all his eighteen-year-old friends. It's wild, great stuff.

In the introduction to On Fire, *you say that the idea of writing was "a curve ball that [you] never saw coming." How did you come to that point where you were going to write seriously?*

After I'd been into it for a year or two...I wasn't really having any success with it, but telling stories was something I really got to enjoy. I got to thinking this was something I'd like to do, to try to make a career out of it, do it seriously. I also finally got to a point where I got a little objectivity about my work and I could see that what I was writing was not nearly as good as the writing I admired most. I saw that there was a big gulf between those two places. That was when it hit me that I was going to have to work even harder, that this was something I was going to have to dedicate my whole life to, my whole being to.

You say you work from your memory and experience. Until On Fire, *there doesn't seem to be a lot directly taken from the things you'd see every day as a firefighter. Is that material reserved for something down the road?*

I'll tell you how *On Fire* happened. It came from not being able to sleep at the fire station, kind of late in my career there. Because we'd have so many runs at night, you'd go to sleep for a couple of hours, but then you'd have to get back up. Then you'd go back, sleep a couple more hours, then go make another run. It totally wrecked my sleep. It didn't wreck anybody else's—they could all go to sleep. What would happen would be that they'd all start snoring and I couldn't go to sleep for nothing then.

So one night I got tired of that. I just decided instead of tossing and turning there all night, I was going to get up and make some coffee and write down everything that had happened that day. And that's when it started, 1989 sometime, when I was still there.

It just became—not exactly a diary, but I began to write about some of the other events that occurred over the years. I started finding out there was a whole lot of material there that might be worth enough to try to make a book out of it. So when I finally got up to about a hundred and twenty pages, I sent all those pages to my editor and said, "What do you think about this? Think we could make a book out of it?" And she said, "Yeah." So that's when I started working on it in earnest. It took me about four years to complete.

People have asked me, "Are you ever going to write a novel about the fire service?" and I've considered it. I've written some openings to short stories, but I don't know. One of these days I might decide to use all that stuff.

You seem to enjoy experimenting with form and voice. In your first collection you seemed to concentrate on voice more, as in "Kubuku Rides." By the end of that book you move into a voice that's closer to the ones in your other books. It seems to be a raw version of your own voice in On Fire. *How conscious was this progression, and is it still going on?*

I think there's a lot of liberties you can take in fiction that you really can't take in nonfiction. To me, in nonfiction you've always got to be totally honest about your feelings about everything, but the thing about fiction is you can assume any role, you can take any stand, you can become any character you want to. Finding your voice is what every writer is looking for. I think really it's more a matter of gaining control of the language and assuming authority so that you can assume any voice you want to and become whatever character you want to. I think early on, in any piece of work that that's got to be established. And after I wrote the first two lines of "Kubuku Rides" I knew the voice and I knew that the rest of the story had to be true to those first two lines. And it was one of those where...you remember a while ago when I told you sometimes you get given a story in its complete form. That story was like that. It arrived with a beginning, a middle and an ending. I wrote it Christmas Eve day in 1986, and I didn't do anything for fourteen hours but write that story. It came in one long shot, and when I finished the story, it was basically just like it is today. Just a gift.

Was that an exception? You said that you threw out several hundred pages of Dirty Work. *Do you put that kind of revision into your short stories?*

I do at least three revisions of everything now. The story I published in the *Paris Review* a couple of years ago called "Roadside Resurrection" was the first thing I started writing when I retired from the fire department. But I didn't get that story finished—the initial writing of it only took a week—until September, and I didn't do much else that year but work on that story. It's a long, long story, nearly novella length. I think it went through six complete drafts. I'd work on it, then I'd send it to my editor and she'd work on it, send it back to me and I'd work on it some more. That's the way we work. We send these revisions back and forth and we talk about them. We write notes back and forth until we're both happy with it.

Your story "Boy and Dog" looks to me like something that could've come from your own experience, perhaps during your firefighting years. Did that actually happen?

Well, the reason I wrote that story was because some dogs know not to get in the road and some don't. Sam would've never gotten hit by a car, he just knew better. I've had other dogs killed—over and over and over—by cars in the road because they don't have sense enough to get out of the road.

One day I was driving up the bypass and I saw this dog come walking out of the ditch and there was this Mustang coming down the road about sixty and the dog never looked around, just walked straight into that car—of course it killed him instantly—and I just got this idea. I see something and I think, "Now what if that was me?" or "What if that was my dog?" The way I was working on it was these little short sentences. I didn't write but about a page of them, and they were all behind each other in line as they ought to be, and I said, "Well, why don't I try to change the shape of this and put them one underneath the other and make each one five words long. Make it look more like a poem. That's how that whole thing evolved.

You said once that poetry was the finest form of the language. Do you still write poetry? How successful do you find yourself at that?

I've been writing poetry ever since I started writing. I've never published any of it. I keep getting asked to show some of it to some of my friends who are poets, whose work I respect, but I haven't spent as much time working on it as I have with fiction. I think it really has to be given the time that it deserves. I don't think that I'm a very good poet. I might have written a couple of halfway decent poems, but there's no way I'd call myself a poet because I've got so much respect for it. Poems are stories, but the poet has it down to its finest parts, to the most beautiful parts of the language.

Your work is often called "spare" and you refer to it as "dark." Do you consider yourself a minimalist? You've said that you learned from Ray Carver. Do you even worry about that kind of labeling? Do you think of yourself as writing in any certain mode?

Carver was a big influence on me, and when I wrote *Facing the Music* it was really in that mode. But I don't really consider myself a minimalist. One of the things I tried to do in *Joe* was describe the landscape in a way that it was kind of a natural backdrop for all the events to unfold against, and it was a constant thing. I always wanted to remind the reader how everything looked and I tried to use my descriptive abilities to the best of my talent. And that book is vastly different from *Dirty Work,* which is vastly different from most of the short stories I've done. But I think that's because you try to do something different each time. You don't want to repeat yourself, keep doing the same thing. And I've discovered that the stuff I'm working on now is different from what's gone before. I hope. I'm trying to develop it more and get it right whenever I'm trying to tell something. There's so many different things you can do with the language. You're unlimited.

Do you always have a character in mind when you start a story?

I'll start with a character in a situation. Sometimes it might be kind of vague what the situation is, but just by writing and developing the character you discover what the story is day by day. If you live with it, carry it around in your head long enough, it's like these people come to stay in your head. Walter and Braiden lived in my head for about two and a half years and I knew the novel was finished when I had helped them as much as I could and there wasn't anything else I could do for them in the story. When the story was over I had to turn them loose, but it was like saying good-bye to two friends because they lived with me all that time. There wasn't a day that went by when I didn't think about them. That's the way it becomes.

How do those situations develop out of the characters?

A lot of people have problems functioning in the ways that they ought to. My characters usually know the difference between right and wrong. They know what the right things are to do, but that might not be what they want to do. It might be because they want to go out drinking or out whoring around instead of staying home and keeping a job and working. And they've all got some kind of struggle, because if you don't lay some kind of trouble on them, if they don't have some conflict, then how are you ever going to have a resolution or an ending. What you've got to do is make things on them as tough as you can and that's what I consciously try to do. I do what I call "sandbagging" and make things as hard on them as I can so then I'll see how they're going to react and what's going to happen and what the story's going to be about.

I think that people in fiction have always got to have reasons for doing what they do. Somebody who pulls out a gun and goes into a bank and robs it has got a reason for doing that. You may not know those reasons. Or somebody's going to rob you, take your money and maybe shoot you: there's plenty of reasons for them to do that, too, but you may not know those reasons. In fiction you've really got to know why the people do the things that they do and you've got to give them some motivation for acting the way that they do. That's another thing I tell my students: He does this or she does this, but why? We don't know why she left him or why he had this wreck, but we've got to know. You've got to explore your characters, and that's how you get your reader involved in your story and characters. People ask me what I think is more important, character or plot. I say character. If you create an interesting enough character, the story is naturally going to follow.

Are there any new writers you're interested in?

One of the best I've seen come along in a while is Chris Offut. There's another guy named Thom Jones who wrote a book called *The Pugilist at Rest.* I'm pretty crazy about both of them, and I still read *The Best American Short Stories* every year.

I met a writer named Tim Gautreaux down in New Orleans one night at a book signing down there and his name just rang a bell. I said, "Are you the one who wrote that story about that guy who went around and fixed all those wells in the 1930s and the Depression and met that real mean woman who was gonna kill her husband?" and he said, "Yeah, that's me." I said, "Wow man, I think you're just a really wonderful writer." The guy just came in the bookstore, you know. I hadn't ever seen a picture of him or anything, and we just had this great talk. I think if you just keep your eyes open you'll keep discovering these new writers who are coming up. They're going to find a place to be heard. They're going to have their voice heard.

I've been impressed with some of the talent that I see in my workshops. I've seen a couple of students who came out of Bowling Green—one of them got an NEA grant, that's Andrew McDonald. He submitted a story that was the last one we workshopped in Bowling Green, two years ago. I was on the NEA panel but I couldn't vote on it because they're all anonymous submissions but I recognized Andrew's story immediately from the title. So I had to get up and leave the room. But he got the grant anyway. That shows you that the other people saw his talent, too. And I've had several from that class who've gone on to publish in the literary magazines. I had one girl there, Anne Panning, who'd already published when I started teaching her, already had her book of stories accepted with Coffeehouse Press, called *The Price of Eggs.* Anne is really good and she's working on a novel, she's written a nonfiction book. She really didn't need anything from me except a pat on the back. She had been writing half her life—she was only twenty-six when she published that book. Started writing when she was thirteen.

You seem critical of the academic path to writing and sympathetic to the writer who just throws himself into the art. Do you see problems in the way writing is learned these days?

In my way of thinking, the only thing an MFA will give you is the ability to go out and teach creative writing. It's fine and good to go and study with a professional because that's somebody who can give you an honest, informed, accurate evaluation of your work and try to point you in the right direction. The reason I went was because I was desperate for some help. I had worked for two years on my own and I had knocked on all these doors and nothing was happening. I wanted someone to show me what I was doing wrong. I was writing mystery stories and horror stories and stories about people killing each other over just hatred or little trivial things, and [my teacher] said, "I don't have any problem with the way you construct a sentence, but your subject matter is what you've got to find and these are the people you've got to read and understand." She gave me the *Norton Anthology of Short Fiction* and said, "You start reading 'The Heart of Darkness' and you start reading 'An Occurrence at Owl Creek Bridge' and you start reading 'A Good Man is Hard to Find' and you'll find out what the things are to write about. And she was right.

I've taught in MFA programs, and really, about all I do when I go and teach is give them my opinion about their work and at the same time tell them, "You're going to get your degree, and that's going to get you a job, some income, and that's fine because you've got to have some income cause you're not going to make it on your writing for a long time. But it's completely up to you how many hours you spend locked away in that room, and only the people who write are going to be writers." There's a difference in talking about being a writer and being one.

You mentioned Breece Pancake's book this morning. There's someone the pressure got to.

There's a lot of pressure, and Breece was a good writer. There's no telling what he'd have done if he'd lived. There's no telling what John Kennedy Toole would have written if he'd lived. And Richard Brautigan. A lot of people have succumbed to that, and "92 Days" and "Discipline" are about dealing with all that frustration and what it's like to want something so bad—and you can't have it and you can't have it and you can't have it and you can't have it—but you keep on after it. I guess it's about the perseverance required to be a writer. "Discipline" was something I dreamed up one day and thought it was an idea that hadn't been tried on before, so I just invented all this stuff. Hack's Prison, these guys going on parole for plagiarism, for copying William Faulkner under the bed sheets at night with a flashlight and stuff. They had to have involuntary sex, they had to put on earplugs and nose plugs and blindfolds, with these obese women who were hairy and sweaty and were whispering, "We're big fans of yours" and told them they were famous and they belonged to a poetry society, and that was his punishment. They wouldn't give him a beer and he had to have this involuntary sex, and this guy was grilling him.

I don't know if you could call it a story. It's more of an exercise, an experiment in form.

How was that one received when you sent it out?

It wasn't received worth a shit. Nobody would take that story, and it was one of the ones I'd sent out so much I finally gave up on it, and then after I had published two books, and was putting *Big Bad Love* together, I had a bunch of other stories I hadn't had published and I showed them to Shannon, and that was one of the ones I showed her and she said, "Oh we've got to publish this." It finally found a home, but no magazine ever took it.

Do you feel your apprenticeship was unusually frustrating or long?

I probably thought it was unusually long, but it probably wasn't really out of line with anybody else's apprenticeship. The only thing that really bugged me was getting to that point in 1985 when I'd written *Facing the Music* and people were telling me, "This is a good story and it's publishable, but we can't publish it. Somebody's going to publish it, but we can't." It was two years down the road before it finally got taken, and then I learned the hardest lesson of all, that you can get to the point where you're writing publishable fiction and still have it rejected for other reasons. It wasn't being rejected because the story wasn't good, it was being rejected because it hurt people too bad to read it. Because it was too honest. And too brutal, some say. And the only way I can really defend myself against any of that is to say, "Well, yeah it's brutal, but I think that it's honest." And what I think you've got to do is share this experience with these people. That's what I'm writing about. That's what the story is about. And you can't just tack a happy ending on things.

1995

ABOUT THE INTERVIEWER: **Michael S. Manley** lives in Chicago. He was editor-in-chief of *Sycamore Review* at the time of the interview.

WAR | FEAR | DREADFUL SHORT STORIES AND GHASTLY PLAYS | ROBERT PERSEVERANCE | OLEN CONSCIOUSNESS | BUTLER THE ARTIST AND THE THEOLOGIAN | THE DIALECTIC

Robert Olen Butler

War, Fear, Dreadful Short Stories and Ghastly Plays, The Artist and the Theologian, The Dialectic

Robert Olen Butler has written eleven novels and five volumes of short fiction, *Tabloid Dreams, Had a Good Time, A Good Scent from a Strange Mountain*, which won the 1993 Pulitzer Prize for Fiction, *Severance*, and, most recently, *Intercourse*. He has published a collection of his lectures on creative writing, *From Where You Dream* and has won two National Magazine Awards, one of them along with *Zoetrope: All-Story* for his story "Fair Warning," which he subsequently developed into a novel. He teaches creative writing at Florida State University.

You have given voice to—I believe honestly—an important part of America, and articulated the craft of the short story. I don't know if you realize that you have helped others in articulating their experiences—experiences I, for example, was not sure others would listen to. What drew you to these complex voices and stories?

My knowledge of the Vietnamese and their culture was, on one level, created from the gift of language. When I was gobbled up in the pre-lottery draft and sent through certain Army schools on the way to Vietnam, one of the stops was a full year of language training in Vietnamese; I spent seven hours a day, five days a week with a Vietnamese native learning the language. So I spoke fluent Vietnamese from my first day in the country, and I had the opportunity and the temperament to seek out the Vietnamese people in their culture and all its variety.

I spent five months working in the countryside and seven months working in Saigon, where I worked in a civilian-clothes job as an administrative assistant and linguist at Saigon City Hall. And my favorite thing in the world was past midnight, almost every night of the week, I would wander out of my hotel and into the steamy back alleys of Saigon—where nobody seemed to sleep—and I'd crouch in the doorways with the Vietnamese people, who, as a group, were the most friendly and open and warm and generous-spirited people in the world, and invariably they'd invite me into their homes, into their culture, and into their lives. I had wonderful friends, from my favorite leper beggar on the streets of Saigon to the highest government officials. So I was deeply immersed in that culture, and in the lives and the individual hearts and souls of those people, and I understood them as well as anyone I grew up with.

On one level that's the answer. But on another level, I have to say that this is a leap of faith that all artists take, that ultimately the artist finds her way down to the deepest place where she discovers, or he, that we are neither male nor female, we are neither Vietnamese nor American, we are neither Palestinian nor Israeli. We are human—we are universally human—and that's the place all artists seek and hope to find. And those surface differences that seem to divide us so profoundly are the things that are the artist's job to leap over, which even include matters of race, ethnicity, culture or gender. And I think it's interesting to note that no one has ever doubted the artist's imaginative ability to leap over barriers that, I personally think, are even greater than gender or culture.

For instance, I grew up in a family where I was an only child, and my mother and father were demonstratively loving, to each other and to me (and they are still together after nearly sixty years). I think it is a greater imaginative leap for me to write about a character who's a white, Anglo-Saxon, male American who comes from a large broken family where nobody ever said the word love, than it would be for me to write about, for instance, a Vietnamese woman who came from a family where she was an only child and her parents were demonstratively loving to each other and to her. But nobody would ever question the artist's ability to make that imaginative leap—and I think it's an even greater one—and artists do that all the time. But this is why art survives, this is why we can be deeply moved by a Sophoclean tragedy two and half millennia old. The artist touches aspects of the human spirit that are universal and defy the surface differences between us, between people.

You stated, long before A Good Scent From a Strange Mountain *came out, that you spoke the Vietnamese language fluently, but that it didn't influence your prose writing. However, your stories do capture a rhythm and syntactic structure that sounds like language in translation.*

That subtle spin on language in most of the stories in *A Good Scent From A Strange Mountain,* I don't think would bear up under any kind of scrutiny in revealing Vietnamese syntax or grammar or whatever. This is an artistic creation. I'm beholden to that kind of veracity. The characters' linguistic spin in their voices is not one that I think is very common in the Vietnamese that I know. But I'm beholden to the higher truths of artistic creation, and so it is enough that even the Vietnamese recognize themselves in these stories. Interestingly enough, on this book tour I was on from January to March of '94, I had a wonderful lunch down in Little Saigon in Orange County, in Winchester, California, organized by a Vietnamese man who's translating *A Good Scent From A Strange Mountain* for publication in the Vietnamese community, and I had lunch with a dozen of the top members of the cultural community in Little Saigon, which is, in essence, the de facto capital of the Vietnamese in America. These were Vietnamese novelists, poets and journalists, and they were all thrilled with *A Good*

Scent, and the thing they were most appreciative of is that the stories treated the Vietnamese as real human beings, not for the book's cultural veracity or its linguistic truth to their own Americanized voices, though often they said that they couldn't understand how I understood the Vietnamese culture so well, and that if they had not known they would have sworn that a Vietnamese had written the stories. I've had Vietnamese react that way to the stories, but the deepest thing is that it portrays them in their fully universal human qualities, which is what they most appreciated. So that linguistic level is open to question. I still don't think that what I understood and the fluency I had in Vietnamese really affected my prose style.

I think it did affect, however, the way I saw the world or the vividness with which I saw the physical world, the sensual world around me, which, when I came back from Vietnam, translated itself into fiction becoming my medium. I went to Vietnam as a playwright and came home a fiction writer, and a fiction writer lives in the moment-to-moment sensual flow of experience, and if you learn a language properly, it's not just a matter of learning the verbal equivalencies of words—you actually rename the world. And the physical properties that we attribute to objects often attend to the words. The difference between an apricot and an umbrella, for instance: at some point those words, the sounds of those words, take on a sense of the physical properties of the thing, and that influence flows the other direction, too. So when I renamed the world with these drastically new names, which were the Vietnamese names, it made me see those things, experience them through my senses with a new kind of freshness and with a different angle. So if the Vietnamese language influenced me at all, and it did, it was not in the way I write my voice but, in fact, in the way I see, in the vividness with which I saw the world in Vietnam.

So that experience may have triggered the sensuality you've been speaking about in the last few days?

It certainly helped to shape that, or intensify it, although I think what I'm saying is that it made me a fiction writer because I believe that all fiction, all literary fiction, at its very heart is sensual. That's the reason fiction exists as a mode of discourse separate from any other: it renders a vision of the world, the order of the world, not through ideas, not through abstraction, not through summary and generalization and analysis and interpretation, but through the moment-to-moment flow of human sensual experience.

I think your collection gives us something that we don't often see in contemporary short stories. The problem lies in the fact that these so-called stories and collections of stories, which tell us how difficult it is to survive in America, are frequently written by a bourgeois class that could afford to enter certain programs and learn this structure of minimalistic writing.

I didn't go through a program. I went through a playwriting program which was a different thing altogether, and I learned my own writing through a long period of trial and error. I wrote five really awful unpublished novels and four dozen dreadful short stories and a dozen ghastly plays—all this written before I ever was published—trying to find my way. And all the while I was in a terrible early marriage and I went to war. As a college student I worked in the steel mills, drove a cab, worked as a business reporter and then as the editor of a business newspaper, in constant contact with people in the business world, and traveling all over the country and so forth.

So I had always been deeply rooted in the working world, and my roots were in this blue-collar, steel mill town in the St. Louis area, and then I was ravished by this other culture, so that's where I learned to write: from life itself. And then through the trial and error of working through the wrong impulses that young writers almost always have—that is, to write from the head instead of the place you dream from, or to write about characters as static, in terms that they have problems but that they don't have a dynamic yearning, which is really what fiction is built on. So I came out of all that.

I think that many times what is lacking in stories, what we criticize in that way that you mention, is the notion of yearning that comes from a life deeply lived, full of moment-to-moment human yearning. Instead, the story comes from the mind and the intellect and ideas, and from the impulse to keep the world at arm's length and to have a literary reputation and to be published—a lot of issues that don't have to do with the creation of art, but rather the creation of an artist. And I find minimalism an inappropriate term because in a lot of these stories not only is yearning missing, but even any legitimate connection to feeling, any sense of that deep undercurrent of human passion. As a result, instead of minimalism—and all art is minimalistic in the sense that it very selectively takes out details and compresses them and gives them back as if they were experience—what we have is sentimentalism.

Now on the surface that may seem an odd term because most of the so-called minimalistic writing seems so hip and so cynical and conscious of things, but with emotion so deeply buried as to be invisible, with yearning not clear or truly there, with the attention to the surface detail and to the turned phrase and to the gloss and to the compression. All of that is present in the work, and also present is that inevitable moment in those stories where you get an elbow in the ribs saying, "Take this very seriously, this is really important." Well, what is sentimentalism? Sentimentalism is when a work expects of the reader an emotion or a reaction that's bigger, deeper, richer than the thing that's being given to you has earned, and that's exactly what we're talking about here. It's a kind of sentimentalism to dwell on the surface without the deep yearnings and emotional undercurrents present, and then to expect you to take that with great seriousness as art. That's the sentimental impulse, and I think that's where much of that kind of writing ultimately fails.

There's so many ghost stories in A Good Scent. *Is that a Vietnamese cultural element or just something you like?*

That's a Vietnamese cultural element. They have a strong sense of the mythic and the alternate world, the spiritual universe going on around them all the time. They're big believers in ghosts. For instance, the ghosts of their ancestors they must pray for. Most Vietnamese believe this in spite of their religion, it's a Confucian thing really, neither Buddhist nor Catholic, but both Buddhist and Catholic Vietnamese tend to have ancestor shrines in their homes, and they are responsible for five generations of ghosts, of the spirits of their ancestors, and they have to do daily prayers in order to keep those spirits from wandering forever without rootedness in that other life.

You've said that your literary influences were the prophets Daniel, Jeremiah, and Isaiah, the apostle Luke. Are they still so?

Certainly the *King James Bible*, rhythmically, is as much a literary influence as any in my work, and in that sense, I think a lot of writers have been influenced by the *King James Bible*. I certainly felt that stylistically I was.

I ask this because I wonder if there were any clergy in your family, and because in reading the works of Ralph Ellison and James Baldwin—both influenced by religion, Baldwin actually being a preacher—your work also came to me. Mostly, though, because Baldwin had said, "From my point-of-view no label and no slogan and no party and no skin color and, indeed, no religion, is more important than the human being." I find the same sentiment in the flesh and bones of your work. Do you recognize this element?

Yes. I think that the artist and the theologian are in the same business. I think we are dealing with the same questions about the nature of existence, and the profound essence of human life. The artist, in creating stories that resonate of that understanding, is really providing the latter-day parables of the infinite that the embodiment of the Christian religion insisted he was always doing. If you read about Jesus of Nazareth in the central work of that religion, you will find the explicit assertion that he never taught in any way other than parable. And there is a certain way of looking at his life to see it as a self-novel—that is, he arranged his life in a way that could be read as a novel; both the stories he told and the stories he made of his life, all of which are ways of trying to get at a vision of something that is, by definition, beyond our finite powers to understand.

And I think that art does that as well, that art creates these structures—these tales, these stories—that if we hear them in the way that they are intended, directly like a harmonic set up in us, we can begin to glimpse something infinite. In fact, the Bible provides us with the first literary critic. Peter was in the boat after Jesus had spoken in parables, and they went out in the boat on the water and Peter said, "Okay, now tell me what all that meant," and Jesus got really pissed off. That was the first literary critic saying, "Okay, fine, you talk about vineyards and masters and sons. Now what did it really mean in abstract terms?" That's the literary critic's impulse, to say the story only existed to come down to this abstract thing. Then, though Jesus translated it, it was with great reluctance, and he was clearly pissed at Peter for asking such a question. His real answer was, "Let him who has ears hear," and that's, I think, the relationship of the work of art to the reader, that's the essential function of the artist: to find sensual images of little glimpses into this utterly incomprehensible infinite thing that is betokened by life on the planet earth, and we come together in the work of art to thrum to that.

A Good Scent *has many interrogations between characters and also within the first-person narrator, who interrogates himself and the world he sees. Can you explain your use of this interrogation, and if interrogation is the right word?*

Well, I think that in all my work for certain, and implicit in all literary fiction, is a consciousness of self, a consciousness of the physical being, of the flow of emotion. If there is a model for this process I would think it's perhaps more dialectic than interrogative, where there's the external world and then the internal response to that, which then shapes the perception of the external world, which then returns to the internal, and so forth. This constant interplay between the isolated self and the external, which can be the physical landscape, the world or other people. And then there's the interrogation, the dialectic, of the present and the past which is ongoing in all of my work as well. Perhaps the model of the dialectic would be more appropriate, but interrogation serves, too. Each questions the other—the isolated self questions the external world as it's represented in place or in person, and the external world and person always intrudes into the inner self and demands some accounting there; and within the inner self there is the reference to the deeper external past and internal past, which then provides its own interrogation of the present self. Perhaps in that way that describes a process that is always present in all my work, yes, and probably in most fiction.

I know you began in acting but changed to writing. Is part of your characterization grounded in playing a part?

Yes, although "playing a character" is not the way I would prefer to say it. Taking on a character, becoming a character, in a sense. The way I think about writing—in fact, the way I teach writing—is like the difference between the way acting was taught and actors created roles in the early part of the century, and how that was shifted by Konstantin Stanislavski in the Moscow Art theater in the twenties.

Before Stanislavski, the dominant mode of acting was often, with great skill and sharp observation, to take on the external gestures and postures and facial expressions and tones of voice of the character, to create that highly refined surface impression of life. But Stanislavski says no, that's not the way to do it, and what you need to do as an actor is to go into that deep personal sensually-based emotional memory (sense memory), and bring your points of reference, sensual points of reference, into concert with the deep inner sensual emotional points of reference of the character you're creating. And when those things become one, and merged inextricably, then and only then does the external performance emerge and have validity. The thing on the outside then comes from the thing inside; internal first and then the external, as opposed to putting on the external—even with great skill.

That's how I feel about writing. Too often these days, certainly in writing programs, and even in the literature that gets published and praised, too much attention is paid to and the work is created from the outside in instead of from the inside out. The focus is on that glossy, perhaps beautifully and sharply observed surface, but the inner reality, the deep reality of the human condition is not present. And that has to precede the external thing, the created object, in the way I write and the way I teach.

Is the place itself, the setting of the work, important for your writing? Along with your characterization, you create these little worlds that are vivid and that guide us through the story. For example in The Deuce *did you do research for the bus terminal, and is Wabash a fictional setting?*

Well, Wabash is not a fictional setting, it's just a fictional name. It is exactly—I say "exactly" obviously with the deep composted sensual freedom that the artist must have in creating a place—nevertheless, Wabash certainly springs directly out of Granite City, Illinois, which is where I grew up. I lived in New York City for a decade and worked there commuting into the city every day, not through the Port Authority Bus Station but through Penn Station, but I knew that area quite well, and so I was working from a place I knew well, also. But interestingly enough, it was in July, I think, I reached the point where Tony is mugged, or he's just arrived at the bus station, is about to be mugged. And you can play fast and loose with physical buildings and so forth in many ways as a creative artist, but such a clearly public place as 42nd Street and the Port Authority Bus Terminal, though I knew it well, I felt I needed to know it better and I needed to immerse myself in it for this book. So three days later I got on an airplane and flew to New York City, and I spent about five or six fifteen-hour days walking every inch of all that area, and all the places where the Deuce lives and exists in this book, I went back and immersed myself in. And not slavishly then to recreate it, but to use all of that recent sensual information to evoke that place.

In dealing with human truths you cover a vast number of issues and characters. Was the area of your upbringing—St. Louis, Granite City, Illinois—important? I noticed you make references to the Ozarks and, obviously, you have the setting for Wabash close to home. Are your home and any experiences from there important to your work?

Oh, sure. Of course. It's a fascinating part of the country, and an interesting thing about St. Louis is that everybody south of St. Louis thinks it's a northern city, but everyone north of St. Louis thinks it's a Southern city. You don't even have to get past Hannibal for them to think about St. Louis as the South, and there's an interesting collision of cultures there. Granite City had absolutely no racial mix at all, oddly enough, but it had a tremendous cultural mix. The steel mills there, where I worked in particular, were a focal point for that collision of cultures because they drew exiles from the Deep South to Granite City, and they drew exiles from the upper Midwest, and there was a very strong Eastern European community there. And so there was a real confluence and collision of cultures and cultural identities, particularly Southern/Northern. I think that made the duality issue, the search for self and understanding the self as an odd and sometimes uncomfortable mixture of somewhat opposite things, an important theme in my work. Certainly, I think it directly made my interest in and my sympathy for the Vietnamese experience in America more clear, and even the Vietnamese in Vietnam. There is a clear Northern/Southern split, which is mentioned in a couple of the short stories, that the Vietnamese have—that same temperamental animosity towards each other that Southerners and Northerners have traditionally had in the United States.

And just the sensual vividness of that place: the Mississippi River bottoms and the river itself and the steel mills. You mentioned the

Cahokia Mound which is the fascinating burial mound from a Pre-Colombian Indian empire that's right outside of town. You go on top of the mound and there's the steel mill putting out its storm clouds of smoke down the way. There was a time in Granite City, in fact, when there was a drive-in movie in a corn field just a quarter of a mile down the road from the Cahokia Mounds State Park, and it turned into a pornographic cinema. So kids could go out and lie on the sides of these ancient Indian burial mounds containing the bones of Indian kings and the retinue of young women that they had murdered to accompany them to the afterlife, and the teenager could lie there on the side of that mountain and look out across the field to this giant screen with these naked body parts fitting together—I mean, it's a wonderfully rich and intensely varied place. The steel mills themselves were wonderful to work in; difficult work, but the industrial aesthetic has always appealed to me.

So, unquestionably, place is very important to my work and rightly so. It's one of the ways in which we select the sensual cues that are around us. We are always in the presence of hundreds and hundreds of sensual cues we could respond to at any given moment, and only a very few of them actually intrude on our consciousness at any given second. And how are those chosen? Well, they are chosen by our emotional selves. And so the landscape then becomes an important direct expression of our inner lives, because how we pull, what we pull, out of the landscape is dictated by our emotions and therefore an expression of it. Our emotions then shape our perceptions of landscape, and landscape itself then begins to flow back the other way and shape our emotional reactions. So there's another dialectic or interrogation always going on that, I think, is at the heart of human existence and, certainly, at the heart of my work.

All those elements were there in Granite City for the compost, the organic base of your work, but the difference between your work and the sentimental is in what came out to you artistically, not the things that made all the connections, like the mounds with the pornographic theater, the steel mills...

Exactly. The things that came out came not from just the sharp surface observation of place, of the social revelations of surface, but the deeper spiritual revelations of the connection between place and the human spirit. That's where the focus was.

In speaking of home or childhood home, you use the first person narrative in your stories. However, the narrator almost always delivers a story and then we have a story inside the story. Were there any storytellers in your family?

Oh, sure. My mother. Her mother, and her mother's sisters. There was a big family of mostly women storytellers, who I was always fascinated with and carefully listened to.

I know that's an obvious question, but right now, when I'm with other student writers in programs, we do tend to forget that there were these elements of our lives that have some relevance on our work.

Sure. And the first difficulty that young writers have is to overcome their fear of what's most deeply imbedded inside them. You'd think that young writers write in order to explore themselves and to understand their own deepest vision of things, and part of them may want to do that, but for most of them what usually comes out in their writing at first is their even greater desire to keep what's deepest inside them at arm's length and to control it and manage it, and the way to do that is through the mind, the rational mind, to write from that place. So those deep things, the things that really shape them, the welter of passion and loss and fear and yearning and all that stuff, you have to really force them to look at it. The great Japanese filmmaker Akira Kurosawa said, "To be an artist means never to avert your eyes," and that's the fundamental lesson to teach young writers. Because the deep impulse is to avert the eyes, to just not see it, to not look. You know you don't want to look at that.

Some things we've been talking about have religious connotations, and you have spoken of God in the past and what He will give you—was it a godsend to teach at McNeese State and live in Lake Charles?

Yes. I was in a marriage with a woman who desperately needed structured, organized religion in order to cope with her own past and her own life. But my own religious feelings, and I use religious in the most fundamental sense, have been constantly shaped and reshaped and certainly away from, strongly away from, organized, institutionalized religion. But my own deepest conviction includes, without question, a sentience behind the universe, and one that's accessible in some inner way to individuals.

I have trouble not feeling some sense of that when I look at a number of the things that have happened in my life; and going to McNeese was certainly one. And if there's such a sentience, it has a good sense of humor, because what brought me to McNeese was this: after creating my first four published novels—on legal pads, by hand, on my lap, on the Long Island Railroad, commuting back and forth from my home in Long Island to a journalism job in New York—and then, finally, having enough publication credits to find a teaching job, and having been out in the world long enough where I thought that the dangers of that were no longer attendant, I started looking and went to some twenty or so universities that were in places where I thought it might be interesting to live, but that were all over, and I got the same response everywhere which was, "We have somebody. This is a sinecure of some value and we've already got somebody teaching." When I talked to McNeese State University, I talked to my now good friend John Wood, who's director of the program, and we had a lovely rapport, but I got the same answer, that they had a fiction teacher.

But then, three weeks later, John called me and said that he had some unusual news, that the fiction teacher had just left his office, and had informed him that he was leaving McNeese and had decided to go into a seminary and become a priest. So I flew down a couple weeks later, interviewed and got the job. It was certainly an interesting turn of events, and one that, in some part of me, as has been true at other important times of my life, I have trouble not sensing as some kind of plan.

It's interesting that some of the things that were in Granite City—the cultural mixtures and so forth—are also present in Louisiana. They come together and it could be some greater power that led you there, but it's also your hard work to keep persevering. It's like a dialectic.

Oh sure. You know, there are different ways to look at that and they may not be mutually exclusive either, but a lot of things came together. I wrote six novels before the fourth of those six was published as my first, and it was the one of the six that I wrote from the right place—my artistic unconscious and not from my head. In retrospect, I wonder after how many novels, at what point does one get discouraged, and say, "Well this really isn't for me, let me turn my attention to other things," because I was amidst what many would envy as a successful career in journalism. And what are you gonna do, write a novel and put it away? Well, I did that. Okay, how about two? How about three? I got to six novels before something happened for one of them. So, yes, that sense of perseverance and hanging in and so forth—none of this stuff could have happened without that being an important part of that mix.

So young writers just have to continuously write, every day?

Oh, I think any fiction writer has to write every day. You finish a book and you put the book out and after you've licked the stamps, you go start the next book, and it's absolutely essential to persevere. Which ultimately means relinquishing the focus on your success. You don't write in order to be a novelist. You don't write in order to gain fame. You write because you have a vision of the world that needs expression, and you don't even know what it is until you write the books, and that's got to be the end in itself, or there's no reason to continue to write.

1995

ABOUT THE INTERVIEWER: **Fred Santiago Arroyo** is the author of the novel, *In the Region of Lost Names.* He is an assistant professor of English at Drake University. He earned his MA in creative writing at Purdue University.

FRANKENSTEIN | SURFING YIDDISH WEBSITES GENRE LABELS | **MICHAEL** I LOVE LUCY | **CHABON** THE NOVEL AS GOLEM | RESEARCH AND TOO MUCH RESEARCH | NATURAL SENTENCES | CIRCUMLOCUTION | THE BUFFYVERSE

Michael Chabon

Frankenstein, Genre Labels, The Novel as Golem, I Love Lucy, Research and Too Much Research, Surfing Yiddish Websites, Natural Sentences, Circumlocution, The Buffyverse

Michael Chabon is the author of six novels, including *The Mysteries of Pittsburgh*, *Wonder Boys*, and *The Amazing Adventures of Kavalier & Clay*, which won the Pulitzer Prize for Fiction in 2001. He is also the author of two short story collections, *A Model World* and *Werewolves in Their Youth*, and the essay collection *Maps and Legends*. He has been a finalist for the PEN/Faulkner Award, the National Book Critics Circle Award, and the *Los Angeles Times* Book Award, and was the guest editor for the *Best American Short Stories* anthology in 2005. He received his MFA from UC-Irvine and currently lives in Berkeley, California. His latest collection of essays is entitled *Manhood for Amateurs: The Pleasures & Regrets of a Husband, Father & Son*.

The Mysteries of Pittsburgh *is often called a coming-of-age novel. The* Yiddish Policeman's Union *was just nominated for the Hugo, a science-fiction award. How do you react when labels are put on your work?*

Having that novel nominated for a Hugo Award was actually, in a strange way, like an un-labeling. It had been written, sold, reviewed, and already classified as a somewhat odd but still mainstream literary novel by a somewhat odd but still mainstream literary writer. It didn't come packaged with any real visual clues to tell you don't read this if you don't like science fiction, which is the way science fiction and other genres tend to be coded, to keep the unwary from being somehow contaminated by their presence. It wasn't like that at all. So I view [the nomination] much more as an adoption. The Hugo Award is actually given by readers—fans—so for them to reach out toward the book and embrace it in that way felt like the opposite of labeling.

In Maps and Legends *you write, "Anything good that I have written has, at some point during its composition, left me feeling uneasy and afraid." You relate writing to building a golem—the novel as this thing that, if you do it right, might just come alive and kill you. Why do you think this danger is so essential to the process?*

Well, that's what makes it fun. That's why you want to build a golem, because there's always this chance that it might work. But every piece of golem folklore tells you that if they do come to life, they get out of your control. They get beyond your grasp. That's a message and a motif that was picked up by Mary Shelley in *Frankenstein*. It's a very familiar image. And if you tend to think of a novel as being like a golem in some way, you can be assured that if it really comes to life and it gets out into the world and gets loose of you, there's no way of controlling what will happen. That could take all kinds of forms. If you live under a repressive political regime, your words could literally kill you. If you write a novel about a family, there's bound to be a member of your family who takes offense at the portrayal of a character even if you weren't thinking of them when you wrote it.

In *Wonder Boys*, the main character's a writer, and he's a big pothead, and he's always sort of creating chaos and disaster for himself. In creating that character, I was thinking of a couple of writing teachers that I've had over the years. But I went to Finland on a trip for the

State Department. None of my books had been published in Finland. In fact there was this headline in the biggest newspaper in Helsinki—like *The New York Times* of Finland—and it was my picture and this big headline in Finnish. I said, "What does that say?" And they said, "Yankee Genius Totally Unknown in Finland." So I went on TV while I was there, and the interviewer said, "Mr. Chabon, in your book *Wonder Boys*, your Grady Tripp is smoking many drugs and having many women. How 'bout you?"

So there's that sense as you're writing of, if I say this, if I attribute this kind of behavior to this character, people might think that's me. They might think I do that, they might think I think that. We all do it—when you're reading a novel, you keep flipping back and forth to the author photo, and saying, "Well, he has red hair, and the character has red hair." When you ask, *Can I actually write that? Can I put this in this book and have people know this or think this about me?*...that to me is a guarantee that you're on the right track.

Sometimes it works differently. You said you've gotten mail from people wondering where they can find original Joe Kavalier art, or saying they've been to Alaska but never noticed all the Jewish artifacts there.

That's a phenomenon that's been creeping up more on me over the years since *Kavalier & Clay*. Because the way *Kavalier & Clay* is written is with this false, omniscient, almost encyclopedic narrator who seems to have full grasp of all the history of the twentieth century, who uses footnotes and always maintains this tone toward the reader that this is all true. That's a very traditional tone for a novelist to adopt, going back to all of those novels that start with the name of the town turned into a dash, or the year is a dash. That promise the novel is making—the false promise—from the very beginning that everything you are about to read actually happened, I used that same approach to *Kavalier & Clay*. And because of that, and because I intertwined real-life characters—Salvador Dalí and Orson Welles—some readers had a hard time sorting out just what was true and what was false. And in fact, that was exactly what I wanted to have happen. I didn't really think it would happen.

I had that experience reading a really good novel called *The Mambo Kings Play Songs of Love* by Oscar Hijuelos. He has these fictional brothers who have a mambo orchestra in New York in the

1950s, and they cut this record. They have this legendary appearance on *I Love Lucy* where they play cousins of Ricky's who come from Cuba. [Hijuelos] describes the whole episode, and at a certain point you start to feel like, "I kind of remember that episode." After I was reading it, I went into a Latin music store in San Francisco and I actually had the thought of wanting to see if they had that Mambo Kings record. And then I was like, "Oh wait, it's fictional. Never mind." I wanted to create that same sense in the reader of *Kavalier & Clay*.

You've talked before about how Fountain City *was sort of a kitchen sink novel. But your other novels are expansive, too. They take a lot of research, a lot of planning. For you, what's the right balance between research and invention?*

Doing the research is one of the reasons I like to write novels. I've always been curious about the Khazar Empire and the medieval Caucasus area, or the history of chess, or comic books, or the Yiddish language. These are subjects that I find interesting, and part of the reason I want to write novels about them is because it will give me the chance to educate myself about them. To have that excuse handy, to spend all this time in libraries just going through old magazines and surfing Yiddish websites, is fun. I like to do it.

Of course, it is necessary. You do make very important discoveries in the course of doing research, and often, especially when you're not quite sure what you're looking for, you find things that totally change the course of what you're writing. For example, in *Kavalier & Clay*, I was sitting in the basement of the Bancroft Library on the Cal campus and going through bound back issues of *The New Yorker* magazine in the years that my novel was taking place. Just looking for anything—what movies were playing, what people were talking about, what they were thinking about. And I found this "Talk of the Town" piece about this researcher for G.E. who was doing research on lightning strikes at the Empire State Building. He was up there every night all summer long with all of his instruments, taking readings. I loved the idea of this lonely guy up there on top of the Empire State Building all night long getting struck by lightning. Eventually, that turned out to be just what I needed for *Kavalier & Clay.* [The novel contains a love scene in the midst of a lightning storm on top of the Empire State Building.]

That being said, research is also a trap. First of all, you can always justify research to yourself, even when you don't need to. I find this particularly insidious on the Internet; if I have an Internet connection, I try to sever it when I'm actually trying to get work done. The other problem is that the more research you do, the more you start to feel beholden to the facts, and I think that's a really dangerous thing for a fiction writer. The more you know, the more unwilling you become to make things up. You'll find yourself saying things like, "I really need there to have been a green bus on the streets of Savannah, Georgia, in 1938, but everything I've researched tells me the buses were all yellow." I think one thing about research that has been the hardest for me to learn is how important it is to abandon it.

I read that, in The Yiddish Policeman's Union, *you purposefully kept your sentences short, almost clipped, compared to your other work. And in* Gentlemen of the Road, *you went the complete opposite direction, sort of consciously overwriting it. Can you talk about your relationship with language, how you approach the sentence- or line-level aspects of craft?*

I have a natural sentence, the sentence that I hear when I'm trying to tell a story. That sentence tends to be longish and it tends to have a lot of parentheticals and dependent clauses, and I like to use threes. I'll often use three adjectives or give three examples or I'll even use three similes, one right after the other, for the same thing. That is not intentional; it's just the sentence form that feels right to me. But it's also a habit. On second and third draft, I'll go in there and force those sentences to justify their form, justify their existence. I'll look at them and try to break them up and put them into different patterns, hear them in a different way. I had to do that a lot more with *Yiddish Policeman's Union*. It got to the point where I was actually frisking my sentences up against the wall as they emerged. I would write the sentence and pat it down to see whether it was holding anything. I wasn't going to waste time with sentences if they weren't going to work that way, which was more clipped, more compact.

I finished *Yiddish Policeman's Union*, turned it in to my editor, and three days later, I started writing *Gentlemen of the Road*. It was being serialized in *The New York Times*, and they needed it in six or eight weeks. With that, I just took off, turned off all the controls, just let it go. I think the sentences you see in *Gentlemen of the Road*–that's like my naked prose. That's how it comes out naturally, unfettered, because I was writing really fast, trying to get it done. The sentences in that book are very long, very tangled. I like circumlocution. Circumlocution is one of those things we're taught to avoid by our English teachers, and rightly so, but I think it's actually capable of very beautiful effects, as well. You force the reader to engage with what it is you aren't saying.

You've written a novel, The Final Solution, *and done some work in comics and film that required you to write preexisting characters instead of ones entirely of your own creation. How is that a different process?*

You know, it isn't, really. I really feel that, ultimately, all fiction is fan fiction. Even in creating your own characters, when you make them up entirely out of your own experience, you're not basing them on Buffy or Willow but on actual, real live people. The way that you approach creating characters and telling stories is determined by the reading that you've done, whether it's Dostoyevsky or Arthur Conan Doyle. I've always seen writing as an act that puts me into play with the people whose work I love. When I was ten or eleven years old, the first story that I wrote was a Sherlock Holmes story, because I loved Sherlock Holmes. And in writing that first story, I felt as if I were being admitted into a game. That there was this game that all the writers I loved were playing, and I wanted in, and the easiest, readiest way that I could imagine doing that—and I think this is the impulse behind the writing of fan fiction—was by adopting the voice and the characters of Arthur Conan Doyle and writing my own Sherlock Holmes story. The same thing with Sherlock Holmes in *The Final Solution*. I didn't violate any precepts of the canon or the things that are known about Sherlock Holmes. But I still tried to fully invest the character, and tried to approach it as if I were making him up for the very first time.

I'm really still trying to get in on the game. All writers are in dialogue with each other. In the Buffyverse or the *Star Trek* universe, there is this sort of shared, collective enterprise going on. To me, literature is just a bigger, broader shared universe.

2008

ABOUT THE INTERVIEWER: **Brian Beglin**'s fiction has appeared in *Artful Dodge* and *The Cincinnati Review*, and his book reviews appear semi-regularly on *The Rumpus*. He is the recipient of a 2009 AWP Intro Journal Award. He lives in Seattle. At the time of the interview, he was an editorial assistant for *Sycamore Review*.

THE METABOLISM OF THE
SHORT STORY |
FICTION SINCE 9/11 | **LAN**
BREAKOUTS | **SAMANTHA**
THE MYSTERY OF **CHANG**
NON-CRAFT | SALT
MINING | NARRATIVE
SHAPES | THE DEATH
TRAP OF POINT OF VIEW
| CHOOSE YOUR OWN
ADVENTURE

Lan Samantha Chang

Fiction Since 9/11, Choose Your Own Adventure, Breakout Sections, The Metabolism of the Short Story, What Makes an Ending Feel Right, The Death Trap of Point of View, The Mystery of Non-Craft, Narrative Shapes

Lan Samantha Chang's fiction has appeared in *Atlantic Monthly, Story* and *The Best American Short Stories 1994* and *1996*. She is the author of *Hunger*, a collection of short fiction, and *Inheritance*, a novel. She is the recipient of the Wallace Stegner and Truman Capote fellowships at Stanford University. She also received, from the Iowa Writers' Workshop, a Teaching-Writing Fellowship and a Michener-Copernicus Fellowship. Her many awards include a Guggenheim Fellowship, and she was a finalist for the *Los Angeles Times* Book Prize. She lives in Iowa City, Iowa, where she directs the University of Iowa Writers' Workshop.

You have categorized yourself as a writer who writes from emotion rather than ideas. Could you talk a little bit more about the challenges of being an emotional writer and the ways in which you think "emotion writers" and "idea writers" differ?

I'm thinking about John Gardner and how in his book, *The Art of Fiction*, he talks about the way he considers *The Iliad* to be superior to *The Odyssey*, and he talks about the way that he considers works based on energic narratives to be more powerful than works that are idea based. Now I don't think that I can go as far as Gardner to say that I think that works based on the potential of the character or the moment are more powerful than works based on ideas. But I do think that there is a distinction that can be drawn between types of writers who are inspired by works that spring from emotion, and in some ways, character, and writers that are inspired by ideas. Of course, some people have both in their work: I'm thinking about this wonderful novel, *A Fine Balance* by Rohinton Mistry, that has this kind of wonderful Victorian setup in which all of the characters begin to represent things, and then they must in some way come together at the end in the way that an elaborately plotted, thought out, sort of mentally inspired novel has to be. But, the characters in that book are allowed some reign over the book and the emotions that are raised by their plight and their growing affection for each other; that also seems to be the heart of the book.

So, I don't mean to say that there are two kinds of books; but in some ways, I think that right now I often notice when I read that a book seems to be working on a set of ideas, in particular, ideas related to current events. If you haven't noticed, a lot of the fiction written since 9/11 is really based on a lot of research. People are doing a lot more research than they did when I was coming up. Then, on the other hand, there is someone like me who has strong feelings about characters and then has to do research in order to make those feelings take form.

Are the characters of Junan and Yinan from Inheritance *born of a particular emotional experience or are they born of an idea: creating two characters, two sisters, very different from one another?*

That book is based on the emotions that I had about the created characters of Junan and Yinan. I was trying to write a book that was set in China. I had some rough idea about what I wanted to have happen in the book that never changed for the whole time I was writing the book. But I couldn't get going on the book until I did character sketches of those two sisters. What viscerally attracted me to writing about them, I think, was my experience as a sister. I have three, I'm an older sister and a younger sister because I'm in the middle, and I've had the experience of being just tyrannized over, and also being in a position of responsibility. I've also grown up really aware of the kind of power that people have over each other, because my two older sisters are very strong-minded. And so, I had heard a story about a sister who basically set up her *meimei*, her younger sister, with her husband because she couldn't get away from where she was, and wanted to keep him in the family, so to speak, and the story grabbed me enough to try to really think about what kind of characters these people would be. So I think that that novel wouldn't have been written if the two characters hadn't come to life in my, I don't know, spirit—that part of you that is taken by things, taken enough to write about them.

In a talk you gave about the writing of Inheritance, *you mentioned that it almost felt like a* Choose Your Own Adventure *because you were drafting so many different versions and exploring all the different possibilities for your characters. You also mention in that talk something about the breakout sections of novels. I was curious about these breakout sections that you talk about and—correct me if I'm wrong—how these breakout sections give the novel an element of unpredictability that transforms the novel into something more expansive and enduring. Can you talk about that here?*

I don't think I used the word "unpredictability." This breakout idea came from a lecture that I gave to Warren Wilson College MFA students. It's this wonderful program in North Carolina where you only get to see your students for a couple of weeks and so you unload what knowledge you have to the large group during that week and then work individually with students.

When I wrote the talk, I was thinking about the difference between novels and short stories, particularly because I was in the middle of trying to work on one myself. And I was stuck because what I had done was almost finish the exposition of the novel, which during the writing of novels I came to understand meant that I had given the reader most of the information they needed in order to finish. And I had a massive trouble trying to finish. I couldn't figure out how the novel should end. I couldn't even figure out where these characters should be or what they should do. I had described this dilemma that had existed between the two sisters and the predicament and I had managed to work in all the information about the Sino-Japanese War, and I just couldn't figure out how to make it end. And, you know, up until that point the longest piece I'd written had been 100 pages and I had also written a number of short stories, and I had no experience in trying to reel it all back in a larger work, and it seemed to me that it might help to think about the difference between short stories and novels. What I realized when I did some reading is that many writers have trouble finishing their novels. They have trouble coming to an end that works, and we've all read novels that disappoint, and we don't want to name them to be rude, but you know what I'm talking about. You get really into it, you get into the world, the exposition grabs you as a reader and then you're stuck with an ending that feels somehow wrong.

So what is it that makes an ending feel right? And to answer that question I have to sit and think: What do novels do? The fact is that novels do something fundamentally different from what short stories do because they take you into a world that you don't know how you're going to get out of. In a short story as a reader, you start the story and you know you're going to be finished in about half an hour to an hour or less. And it's something that's built into the metabolism of a short story—that it's short—and there is an expectation of a finish for the reader. So you could even say that it's possible that readers go to short stories because they know that they're going to be finished in a short period of time, that they're going to have a complete experience. Whereas people enter novels, I think, for a different reason. They go to novels because they don't want to know that they are going to be finished. They want to get lost. And getting lost is where the whole idea of the breakout came into my mind, which is that a novel implies—I mean a novel, this sort of creation of the world, the time and energy spent describing the minutia, the slower pacing, the large amount of exposition that goes into most novels—all of that implies that the writer is creating a world, and as a reader that's one of the wonderful things about novels. But the real world doesn't come to an end; the real world doesn't have to conclude itself, and so a novelist is stuck with this strange problem that they created a false idea—that you're reading a world that's like our experience of being here—and yet they have to tie everything together and finish it. The idea of a "breakout" is that most novels that end up coming up with successful endings have a moment in which the structure or the characters or some element of the novel goes out of what you'd expect. And I think this is probably why a person describing my talk used the word *unpredictability.* So there is something that becomes different than what you've been lead to believe, and it's that break that gives the reader the sense that the world of the novel—oh here it is—is as unpredictable as our world. So a lot makes us feel as if we've really entered another world.

Example: *A Fine Balance* by Rohinton Mistry. There is a character in the book called the Beggarmaster. This is an obscenely long book; the Beggarmaster shows up on page 237—it could be page 137, I don't want to be wrong in your journal, I might have the number wrong, but it's way in there. He shows up and he comes in like this kind of Mafia character, this overlord type or underlord type who has control over the lives of these poor beggars who are in this predicament. And he speaks in this sort of slightly clichéd language of the underworld. And, he's enjoyable, and he seems almost flat—this is in his first appearance. And then as the book continues the tone changes remarkably in this fascinating way, and it's mostly due to this character, his character's influence over the other characters, and also the way the character grows and deepens and becomes much, much larger than life.

I wish that I had time to go into this at length because it's completely fascinating. Read the book and see the way the character develops, layer by layer, becoming more and more large until the second half of the book, and especially toward the end of the book, he really dominates the world in which the four main characters exist. He becomes a symbol of not just a corrupt person, but somebody who sort of discovers his humanity. He finds out that he's a brother to the most decrepit beggars; he has a spectacular demise. And he really becomes this almost surreal character. But to me, the book starts off in this fairly straightforward fashion by bringing our four characters together in the first bit, putting them into a room together, and then the three backstory sections, flashbacks, that take you into how they all got into the situation one at a time, because two of them are relatives and so their stories are done together. And then we move on into the rest of the book, and up until then it all seems fairly realistic. And then, at a certain point Beggarmaster enters and the entire book changes. I think the book becomes a very, very, very large—and I don't mean because it is 600 pages—it becomes large because the world becomes large, and the world takes on these enormous moral issues. It's that that makes the book outstanding and huge. That's what makes it work as a novel.

The funny thing about breakouts is they often feel wrong, and this is the thing about them that ultimately makes them work, but also makes the book imperfect. I don't think that there are very many novels that have this glossy sheen of a pearl that Gardner talks about when he describes novellas, or shorter works. I think he actually described it as oriental purity of line, which I found to be a sort of interesting word choice. But they don't have that because they have to be large and messy. That's where the breakout happens.

For me the breakout was a big jump in time. I took an enormous jump. I finally cut out everything that happened between mostly 1955 and the 1970s or 80s or 90s. This was just chopped out. I thought, "I'm just going to jump, I don't think anybody really cares what happened to these characters during that time."

One thing I really admire about Inheritance *is your use of point of view and that Hong is narrating what's happening to the grandmother, mother, and aunt, even before she comes onto the scene. Could you talk a little bit about your decision to use that point of view?*

Well the decision took two years because I was drafting a hundred pages at a time and I decided not to put a restriction on myself for point of view during that time. So I had all these different pages drafted in different points of view. And then I didn't know what to make of the point of view, and I actually had to sit down and figure it out, which is so interesting to me because—have you ever read this book, Janet Burroway's *Writing Fiction: A Guide to Narrative Craft*? Well you know there's like two chapters on point of view in the book and she's so minute about it that you just want to throw the book out the window. I probably only managed to make it through both of those chapters twice. I just can't deal with it, and I thought, "What is the big fucking deal about this point of view? Just write in the point of view you choose." And then I started writing a novel and realized that point of view is this death trap, so you're stuck in your point of view. And I was like, "Oh my god," how do I write about World War II in China and about then the United States, and how do I write from the point of view of people from one generation from another without being omniscient? Because, at the time, I don't think I had the energy to try to write omniscient, and also the book felt too personal for me. Again, these are my own restrictions.

But anyway I was at, believe it or not, MLA in 2000, and I heard them talking about this book *Charming Billy* by Alice McDermott. And I started thinking, "You know, maybe I can write like that." The novel is in the first person but really the first person narrator hardly ever shows up. She never talks about herself. It's all about her uncle and her mother and father, this other woman. I thought maybe I could do that. But I started reading books and realized that most first person books have a part where they breakout of first person.

I'm interested in texts that deal with public stakes and private stakes, novels that deal with the global, historical, and political while allowing us into the private lives of compelling characters. How do you write about larger political issues without becoming didactic or without running the risk of weaving away from the narrative?

Well, this is wildly related to the question of point of view. It's very interesting, you know, it's really interesting. So then you start to think, "Oh god, I have to sit down and make an executive decision about what point of view I'm going to have." On some level, you sort of do. The decision you make is going to determine the scope of the book, the tone of the book, the voice of the book, that's the key thing. The other thing I realized about novels in the last ten years, which I haven't been able to put into practice in my own work, is that voice is everything in a novel. Nobody wants to read a novel if they don't have confidence in the authority of the voice. So you're screwed if you can't find a voice. Most novelists spend a lot of time mucking around looking for a voice, but most novelists who write more than one book in their lives run into this. I talked to one really famous MacArthur-winning novelist whose name I won't mention because I don't know if she'd want me to talk about it, who mucked around for years trying to find the voice for her latest book, even though she'd written a million books before. It was horrible; she said it was just like digging relentlessly in the salt mines.

Reza Aslan, a University of Iowa graduate and the author of No god but God, *mentioned in an interview that one of the most important things that he learned during his time at Iowa was the discipline of writing. Do you think discipline can be taught, and in your own experience—because it took you a long time to write* Inheritance*—how did you handle those days when the words just weren't coming?*

First the idea of learning discipline at Iowa kind of cracks me up because we hold—well the thing about our program which I think makes it special after all these years is it's a fairly pure descendent of the original MFA program. So what that means is that we give the students there an enormous amount of time to write. We often try to make sure that they're exposed not only to the academic element of writing such as the teaching of craft that has become much more prevalent now than it was when writing programs first started out, but also that kind of mystery of non-craft. This sort of "What's making this work? We have no idea," feeling that comes sometimes for writers. So there is a deliberate attempt to make sure that people don't believe that there is some kind of answer that can be gleaned in a nuts-and-bolts way, as well as the teaching of craft. Giving them a lot of freedom is part of it. I suppose that if anyone learned discipline from all this, it would be because they realized nobody is making you write except for yourself. Probably, that's what Aslan meant. You're expected to just hammer out your writing, and you're given an enormous amount of time with which to do it, and you're not told how you're supposed to write.

One thing I learned through the experience of writing my novel is that I had this tendency to start something long and then give up. Finally I decided to try an in-between length and that's how I came up with the novella "Hunger." The challenge of writing a 300-plus page work was that I just couldn't understand for a long time that novels are fundamentally different from shorter works. And also that I knew there was a possibility that I would just give up, and so I decided when I was writing *Inheritance* to break it down into hundred page sections. I knew I could write a hundred pages, and so I broke it down into five, and ultimately four, hundred page sections. The rule when I was drafting was that I would write a hundred pages, but I wasn't allowed to look back. So I would do a hundred, and then I would put them away and do the second hundred, and so on, because what I had found earlier was that given the opportunity to look back I would just keep revising the first chapter until it was dead.

I don't know if that's discipline. In my mind it was just a lot of confusion because I had never written something long, and I wasn't a quick study, and I had a tendency to keep revising everything over and over. What I remember most about this was there was one year when I made some kind of New Year's Resolution—it was 1998, the year *Hunger* came out—that I would write ten pages a week for the whole year. By the end of the year, I thought then I would have theoretically 520 pages of a draft. I ended up with 450 pages because I had major surgery in the middle of the summer and because I had to take off for several weeks while *Hunger* was coming out to go travel, but that's what I did that year. I don't think of it as much as discipline as just this kind of desperation and drive and the sense that I didn't know what I was going to do after *Hunger* came out, because I'd been working on the stories for *Hunger* for so long that I felt this enormous void coming at me. And so I decided that I had to fill it up with yucky pages from my novel. The interesting thing about those pages is that of course I threw away a huge number of them, but there were parts that came out of order during that time and are important parts in the novel that are basically verbatim.

So you're writing a number of novellas. Are these going to be turned into novels or are you going to stick with them as novellas?

I want to put the three stories I'm working on about one family in a book together. So, that's sort of a project I'd like. I applied for a Guggenheim Fellowship and I got one for this year. I'm taking it in two parts because of the responsibilities of my job, but the project that I used to apply was three parts about the characters Ming [mother], Sansan [father], and Charles [son]. Sansan's is basically drafted but I know there is something wrong with the first half. So the question is, when on earth am I going to figure out what's going on in Charles's mind? The other piece that I'm working on is about a poet; it is now about 150 pages and I just finished a draft. And I think that's going to stand-alone; it's not related to anything else I've ever written and I don't know what else would happen to it. That is merely a draft. The only project is the one that's the biggest mess and I'm sort of just waiting to see what happens to it. This family piece about this restaurateur and illegal immigrant.

You have mentioned that in your first book, especially the story, "The Unforgetting," you were really interested in the idea of assimilation, but that now you're approaching theme more subtly. So I—

Did I say that?

Something to that effect.

Oh yikes! I don't think I'm more subtle than I used to be.

So I guess my question is how has your relationship to theme changed over your career?

I can't answer that question. I never think about theme. I think "The Unforgetting" is the only story from that book in which I might've even thought about theme at all. And it wasn't even theme. For me, it was just this idea that sacrifice was involved. That people seem to think that all Asian Americans magically became really smart or something. There are a lot of stereotypes, and I thought there was nobody writing about the underside. Just being able to do well in school or become part of a "successful American culture" didn't tell the whole story.

So it's not something that you think about at all in the drafting of the story?

I really don't. I don't have any issues with theme: I think this is the idea of writing from ideas. If that's what makes you write, I would never take it away from you. It's just that's not where I come from. I start with characters and feelings and then I end up thinking, "Oh, I get it, this is really a story in which memory plays a huge part." But not until I've sort of tromped it out. I congratulate anyone who can be more direct in their work. I can't.

I'm kind of in awe of how you use time in your work; in "Hunger" the novella, a couple stories in there, and Inheritance *of course. They just cover these enormous amounts of time. And I always think that's really difficult to do. I was wondering if you could talk about the hows and whys of that process, and why you use so much time, and how you make that choice.*

I'm sure that I use a lot of time because that's how my mind works. My oldest sister says, "You think too much," and I'm always trying to draw connections between something that my mother did when she was eighteen and something my sister is now doing, you know, that kind of stuff. When I think about a story I'm always sort of thinking about it that way. And also the way people change is of great interest to me. I'm not great at describing exactly the way they are right now, but I am able to imagine them in different times in their lives.

So that leads to a challenge, which is what to do about flashbacks, and what to do about narrative shapes in general. I think that because my mind works that way I've always had to deal with it and that's why I end up pushing stuff together, moving around. I don't actually think I do jump that much; when I jump, I usually jump forward. That could just be having had the idea of forward movement hammered into me when I was at Stanford, or the idea of scenes which usually move forward hammered into me by just reading. And also I think moving forward has a relation—I mean it's basically our human structure, isn't it? We wake up one morning not knowing what's going to happen and then we go through our day. I know what happened to me when I was five but I don't know what's going to happen to me next year. And so I think the time jumps come from knowing what happened in the past and not knowing what's going to happen in the future. So I start back and then I move forward. Occasionally there's a jump back. I think at the end of "Hunger," Min remembers her husband as a young man struggling to get onto a boat so that he could leave China and come to the United States. That needed to be there, and I don't know why. That was something that I didn't write first then put it in later; I actually wrote it when I was finishing the book, like it came, and I knew that I had to go back and explain that and then keep going. I think it's the way my mind works. That's all it is. The way my mind works creates the need to put stuff together. This piece I'm working on now with the poet: it has three parts. The first part takes place when he's in his MFA Program. I know, isn't that appalling? The second part takes place when he's teaching, and the third part takes place when he's so famous he doesn't have to teach much anymore. This is every writer's fantasy. But there are jumps between the sections twelve to fifteen years long, and I just realized I had to make those jumps because the material in between was too boring.

You had a couple published or unfinished stories that you did not put in Hunger—

Yeah.

Why didn't you, and how important was it to you that Hunger *be a thematically linked book? Or is it a thematically linked book?*

I think it's probably thematically linked. The story that I remember the most that didn't go in—I haven't read it in years—was published in *Story Magazine*; it was about a young woman who comes to the United States and works in a restaurant and meets a man. It has a very different tone to it, I'm not sure how to describe the tone, but I know it's very different from what was in the other pieces. I think I probably left it out because it didn't feel like it was the same thing. So to answer your question, I think probably when I put the collection together I was thinking along the lines of wanting the pieces to fit together, not necessarily thematically, but tonally. And then what happened was when the book became a product, it became marketed, and people figured out what the themes were, and I figured out what the themes were. When people asked me about it I would talk about it, because you were supposed to talk about your work in a way so that people would know what the book was about. Those are all the questions that you'd be asked; you know, "Tell me what this is about." Which is really saying, "What are the themes?"

So again, I don't really think thematically. I admire people who do; I just haven't picked up on that. The one that really blew my mind away, which I'm embarrassed to say I hadn't read until four years ago was *The Brothers Karamazov.* Just such an amazing book, I mean a book that I want to go read right now. It's all about ideas; every one of the characters is an idea. And yet the book is so vivid and wonderful. And one of the reasons it's so large is clearly he [Fyodor Dostoevsky] is pitting the ideas of good—and I suppose in his mind Christianity—up against the world, and that's why the book is so large, because he uses big ideas, because he's thinking on that level.

One thing I've noticed in the last ten years or so, or maybe fifteen years, is that the fiction in the United States changed to some extent where there is much of a larger world in it. I think part of that has to do with the way we have become aware of the world, and the world has come to us. There are many more people in the United States now who weren't born here. And so our experience is changed and broadened, and the fiction is changing. What that's doing is changing point of view. People are much more interested in being able to get into more than one point of view now. When I was growing up everyone was writing close third. Do you remember this? It's changing the nature of what people read from sort of these personal narratives—memoirs taking that over—to something more political. I continue, of course, to write personal narratives, because that's sort of what I do, but I enjoy reading the other work.

2009

ABOUT THE INTERVIEWER: **Mehdi Okasi** graduated with an MFA in creative writing from Purdue University in 2009. He was *Sycamore Review's* editor-in-chief at the time of the interview.

WHO WRITES SCIENCE FICTION | THE BOUNDARY BETWEEN FEELING AND THOUGHT | GIANT CRUSHING BOULDERS | PETER BEACHHEAD STORIES | HO CLOSURE | DAVIES HISTORICAL MATERIAL | KITCHEN SINK DRAFTS

Peter Ho Davies

Who Writes Science Fiction, The Boundary Between Feeling and Thought, Giant Crushing Boulders, Beachhead Stories, Closure, Kitchen Sink Drafts, Historical Material

Peter Ho Davies is the author of two short story collections, *The Ugliest House in the World* and *Equal Love*, as well as the novel, *The Welsh Girl*, which was long-listed for the Man Booker Prize in 2007, and short-listed for The Galaxy British Book Awards 'Richard and Judy' Best Read. His work has appeared in *Harpers, The Atlantic Monthly, The Paris Review, The Guardian, Independent, Washington Post* and *Chicago Tribune*, among others. Born in Britain in 1966 to Welsh and Chinese parents, Davies was named by *Granta Magazine* as one of its twenty "Best Young British Novelists" in 2003. He is a recipient of fellowships from the Guggenheim Foundation, the National Endowment for the Arts and the Fine Arts Work Center in Provincetown. He is a 2008 recipient of the PEN/Malamud award. He is now on the faculty of the MFA program in creative writing at the University of Michigan.

I'm sure a lot of your readers are curious about your influences. You mentioned from previous interviews that you were heavily influenced early on by the science fiction of Kurt Vonnegut, as well as a little known British book entitled, Who Writes Science Fiction? *Do you find yourself still frequenting these books even as an adult?*

I often attribute science fiction as the form of fiction that led me to writing. When I was a teenager, I was not a literate young man, so I read almost nothing but science fiction, and as one often does as a young writer, I first wanted to write what I loved to read. Growing up in Britain during the mid-seventies and early eighties, it always seemed to me that writing was what those other people did. Books were written by, for lack of a better phrase, upper- class people who lived in London. That's how I thought about it.

When I was younger, probably the most famous young writer in Britain during that period was Martin Amis. Martin Amis was the son of a very famous British writer, Kingsley Amis, and I thought that was how you became a writer; you were born into this family business. It seemed that you could no more become a writer then you could become the king. You had to be born into the whole deal, like Prince Charles. What was interesting about science fiction and particularly this book you mentioned—in Britain it was called *Dreammakers*, I believe—was that it was the first time I ever thought about the writers behind the books I was reading. Nearly all of the science fiction writers were guys who came from science and engineering backgrounds. They were guys who, because of the nature of science fiction publishing, were writing six books a year. Science fiction writing seemed like a) hard work, and b) fiction that was written from non-literary backgrounds. My father was an engineer, so since I went to college to study physics, it was already easier for me to follow in my father's footsteps. Imagine being an engineer or a scientist and becoming a writer through that track; this was much more imaginable to me than becoming Martin Amis. The fact that these guys worked hard also made it seem less about the muse pointing its finger at you saying, "Yes, that's a brilliant idea, go ahead and write it," and made writing seem more like a job, which was also more imaginable to me.

Vonnegut was important to me as a kind of gateway drug to literary fiction. Once you read Vonnegut's *Slaughterhouse Five*, you were just one removed from *Catch-22*, and once you read *Catch-22*, you were one removed from *The Naked and the Dead*, and once you read Mailer, you were a step away from Hemingway, and once you read Hemingway you were reading everything; you're in the full mainstream of twentieth century literature. Vonnegut was that stepping stone, and even as a teenager in Britain I was reading a lot of American literature. All of those writers that I've just mentioned are writers that, when you read one book by them, you want to read everything else by them, and I think that's very important for a writer.

As my life goes on, I feel as if there are fewer and fewer of those writers. Through my teen years there were a lot of them. In college, I wanted to read everything by John Irving. In recent years, Philip Roth is very exciting to me, and though his work is uneven, there's plenty more to read because he's got a lot of books. J.M. Coetzee is the other person in that category at the moment. When I think about Roth and Coetzee, what's exciting to me about them is their craft. In Vonnegut, I figured out how a paragraph works in novels. Each of his paragraphs serve as a kind of joke, working its way into a punch line. It made me think of how a paragraph is a small narrative in its own right. Hemingway is great for young writers because you suddenly realize it's not about the multi-syllabic words and the adjectives.

But Roth and Coetzee made me think of writing in a different way. They made me question whether I was writing from here (the head) or from here (the heart). I worry that sometimes it might be coming more from my head than from my heart. Roth is a very intelligent and intellectual writer, but that intelligence, particularly when it comes with his anger, seems to press into these great flights of intellectual bravado. When I think about his work, the boundary between feeling and thought seems to dissolve. That's one of the things I admire that I have yet to bring into my own work. I'm not sure how I would do it. It's less of an influence at the moment than perhaps an inspiration.

The Welsh Girl *is your first novel. Before that, you published two collections of short stories,* The Ugliest House in the World *and* Equal Love. *Was there anything in the writing process of* The Welsh Girl *that you did consciously different from writing a short story?*

Certainly one of the things I struggled with a great deal was an aesthetic difference between the novel and the short story. The book took me just about seven years to write and I suspect that if I had been more conscious of some of those differences it might have been a little faster.

Whenever I write a new story, to some extent, however that story may diverge from previous work, I have those past stories as a touchstone. They are previous pieces of writing that worked in some ways, so even when I'm in the midst of new work that is rougher or sketchier, there will be moments when I go, "Yeah, this feels a little bit like my hand when I wrote that earlier story." There's a tendency to measure our product against our memory of previous work. In transition from writing a story to a novel, I inevitably was comparing my novel-in-progress with my past stories, and that's problematic because the way I value stories is different from the way I value novels.

I read a review a few years ago of Zadie Smith's second novel, *The Autograph Man*, which got some mixed reviews. The review I read was more generous, and talked for a chunk about Zadie's first book, *White Teeth*, which the reviewer clearly had loved and spoken of very highly. At one point in the review, she said it was the best British novel since Dickens, but that it falls apart at the end. The review made me worry more about endings, and made me remember back to a number of contemporary novels I'd read and enjoyed a great deal but nonetheless had been disappointed by the endings.

I don't think it is a totally uncommon experience to read a great novel that has let us down in some ways. But I don't believe it's possible to say a short story is wonderful but falls apart at the end. The best you can say is that a story is mediocre and that it falls apart at the end, because a short story lives and dies by its ending. The aesthetics of a short story feels like a geometric shape, a sphere or cube, something I can hold in my hand. I can turn and look at every word, every detail as a contribution to the whole. In those regards, the story can aspire to something close to perfection.

I took some of that aesthetic notion into writing a novel, and it's tricky. You can even make it a point that the perfection I'm talking about in the context of a short story actually has anti-novelistic qualities. We don't want our novels to be perfect. Novels, strangely enough, because they're more like life, are less like art. Stories tend to be more artful, I think, than novels. This is a kind of aesthetic realignment I had to go through. When I think about the novel as an object, instead of the small discreet thing I can hold in my hand, it's a giant boulder that, if I'm lucky enough to pick up, would crush me. If it just sits there on the ground, I cannot look at it all at once. I have to walk around. I can maybe only see one side of it at a time. It's a much harder object to capture.

To me, a lot of that speaks to the ways in which memory plays a part in the reading experience. When you think about reading a short story, you read it for twenty minutes but ideally, hopefully, even in the act of reading the last line, you spend some time in contemplation of the story. Even if that's only five minutes and the story took twenty minutes to read, that five minutes is a significant portion of the reading experience: twenty percent of the whole. With the novel, we spend more time in the actual reading. I read a section a day, I go to bed, go to work, and then I read a little bit more. I'm not sure if we reflect when we finish a novel in quite the same way we reflect after reading a short story. What's essential to a short story is the way we hold it in our memory after we're done, that we can think of it as a whole thing. With a novel, our perception is much more in the way that we move steadily through it, not just after the fact. So I had to think a lot about what makes a good story and what makes a good novel, and it took me three or four of the seven years to start figuring that out.

There is an assumption in the literary world that readers prefer to read novels to short fiction. Do you feel that the current relationship between novels and short stories is a healthy one?

I do think that something of that perception is certainly true in Britain. When I think of the British marketplace, British readers by-and-large do not have access to short stories in the forms of popular magazines like *The Atlantic* or *The New Yorker* or *Harpers*. There's just not that tier of publishing in Britain. For those British readers, they struggle when they read short stories, particularly story collections. They read them as if they were novels, not understanding the differences. Whatever novel they're talking about, whether it be Jane Austen or John Grisham, in some part of the discussion they're going to say they couldn't put it down. There's continuity in the reading experience, a momentum. You could probably argue that one of the reasons why a lot of novels don't end well is because the primary novelistic skill is to keep people reading. So if that's your major skill, then by nature you might not be very good at stopping people from reading further. Short stories, because of their emphasis on the ending, nearly always have an emphasis on closure. I think sometimes the British people, when they read a short story collection, read it as if it was a novel, from one story to another. Really what I'm suggesting is that there needs to be a break between each story during which one reflects on whether or not it's doing its work appropriately.

The Irish writer and critic Frank O'Connor has a book called *The Lonely Voice* about the history of the short story. Now O'Connor is not that great of a critic by any means. Sean O'Faolin compares him as a critic to a man in a shooting range with a machine gun, spraying bullets all over the place, but only hitting two or three bull's-eyes. But in this book, O'Connor has this theory that short stories are written about submerged populations, a weird term that he's probably not comfortable using himself. We might think of that term as people of lower classes, immigrant groups, and we could see a sense that some short stories have come out of these groups.

Imagine that you're a writer or a publisher, and you're writing a short story about a strange and unlikely submerged population group, Albanian transsexuals perhaps. You want to write a short about the group, a story that may take a week or a month to complete, and you send it out and a magazine takes it. The story is only five, ten, or twenty pages, and you've only devoted a low amount of time and low page count to it. It's a lot less risky than say, writing a whole 500-page novel about Albanian transsexuals. If that short story does well, other people decide to discover that territory by writing more short stories, which are low-risk for writers and publishers. Through those short stories, the submerged population group is going to begin to emerge in literature. Novelists may eventually come in and say that's a theme they want to write about. In a way, short stories are like the troops establishing a beachhead, and a novel is like the heavy artillery. So there's a kind of symbolic relationship between the story and the novel. The story is breaking ground for new material that is then reinforced by later novels.

The Welsh Girl *is told from three very different perspectives. Why was it important to tell the story from these distinct perspectives?*

That's a very good question. I asked myself that a good deal in the writing process. The current form of the book, while I'm very happy with it, is a result of both planning and accident because of my writing process. When I was a short story writer, I tended to work in very short and discreet bursts. I'd work on a story for a week or just a weekend, and then put it aside for a long stretch of time. That discreet, interrupted short-burst pattern of writing was fine for short stories, but much more problematic for writing a novel.

By the end of the novel, I was much closer to the other writing model that we often talk about: writing every day. It's very important for a novel. Days when I knew I wasn't going to have very much time, I'd put into the effort by being in touch with the novel as best as I could. Even if I had just half an hour, I'd try to read a couple of pages of the book just to keep all the elements in my mind alive when I wasn't specifically writing. Before I did this, the effect of the early interruption of the writing process was that I would write a chunk of the novel for one summer and then leave it alone for a couple of months, and then come back to it not happy with what I had. I did what I always tended to do, particularly because I was a short story writer: I started somewhere else, did more research, and began in a whole different perspective. Then I'd write that story for awhile, put it aside, and return to it again.

There was a version of the book that I called the kitchen sink draft. It had everything I ever thought about in it, and was two-hundred pages longer than the original finished version. After that version, I decided with my editors to write what I now call the "Slim-Fast Version" of the book, a hundred and fifty pages, which was just Esther's story. That seemed stronger and I liked it more, but my editor in the U.S. said she missed some of the other stuff. She said that although this draft was publishable, she'd wait until I got it right. She had a lot of patience in me and I wrote another version, wove Esther and Karsten's narratives together.

At the very eleventh hour, I decided to reinstate the Hess material. Oftentimes in conversations with readers I get asked whether or not that material, mostly in Prologue and Epilogue now, served the rest of the book. The logical answer I use is that I wanted to provide some background and some scale to World War II while dealing with the foreground of a very intimate story about these people on the fringes of the war. So it would be reasonable to address one of the order-givers, and not just those given the orders. It's also true that by the end of the book I needed that third point of view by which to tell the end of the story of the other two characters. I couldn't effectively tell it in either of the two.

In these different perspectives, you take on different races, different genders. What must a writer do in order to ensure that he or she remains true to a different race or gender?

I'm not sure if there's an easy answer to that. All I say to my own students is that there's a lot of anxiety in crossing these lines of ethnicity, of gender, of class, of sexuality, because I feel that we've all heard of the advice: write what you know. That's smart advice, and at the same time we are also wary of the political appropriation of other people's stories. Actually that anxiety is the key to doing it well. If you're worried about doing it, then you're hopefully going to think up ways of doing it respectfully. What worries me more—and I see this a lot among students—is that some writers think it's so hard to write in another perspective that it stops them from even trying to do it. With everything in writing, we can only learn to do better by trying, so it's worth trying to do it just to explore it. So there's a kind of pitch between letting our anxiety censor us from trying and striving to maintain that anxiety by being as careful and respectful as possible.

Another way I convince myself to write in other perspectives is to think about similarities. I wrote one of my earliest stories from the point of view of an adolescent girl, and I was thinking that although an adolescent girl is very different from an adolescent boy, there are also a lot of ways in which they are similar. Again, sometimes we're so engulfed with the differences of characters that we tend to neglect the points of similarity.

The title of the novel has evolved since the early excerpts. It was called The Bad Shepard *in* Ploughshares. *The current title,* The Welsh Girl, *seems to focus a lot of the attention on one of the three protagonists. But the reader learns very early on that the definition of "Welsh" also has other, surprisingly different meanings beyond that of nationality. Why was it so important to include the 1928 Oxford English definition of the word "Welsh" in the preface?*

For a long time, the book was called *The Bad Shepherd.* In that kitchen sink version with those extra two-hundred pages, most of the extra stuff was about being a shepherd. There was a lot more stuff about sheep in the book than there is now. A lot of things got cut out, and it was a lot less about shepherding and the title seemed less appropriate.

Going back to answer your question about the definition of "Welsh," I feel that, as a fiction writer, I'm attracted to subjects and territories that even the factual records cannot reach. The derivation of the term "welsh" is kind of a derogative notion: to welsh on a bet, to welsh on a deal, to cheat, to steal, to betray. The derivation, as the Oxford Dictionary would tell you, is obscure, and that's kind of interesting. There's this whole slur upon a nation and we don't know where it comes from. It all feels like a space in which fiction can start to provide some of these answers or at least provide possible hypotheses. I wouldn't want myself to pick between the different ways these derivations could have come about, so I put them in the mouths of a couple characters because I think it's the right choice for them, for the way they would think about the word "welsh."

That's probably true of the way I think about historical material in general. When I think about Rudolf Hess as a character, I'm not sure I'd have fictionalized any other figure in the Third Reich because it would just be too problematic, too easy to fall into the falsification of those characters. It seems ethically very problematic. I'm sure my version of Hess is not the true version of Hess, but at the same time, history and biographers do not have access to a "true" version, either. Hess was a man who flew to England in the 1940s and fell into British hands and claimed amnesia. Though some people think it was just a ruse, there's a little worry in me that the verdict is still out that we don't know for sure whether or not he's suffering from a genuine hysteria or some kind of breakdown. When I talk about Hess as being the "hammer" to the Third Reich, we don't know whether his anti-disposition is real or fake. And because history cannot go into that space, again, I think fiction can occupy and offer us some theories.

2008

ABOUT THE INTERVIEWER: **Michael Wang** was an editorial assistant for *Sycamore Review* at the time of the interview. He earned his MFA from Purdue University

SPRINGSTEEN, TOM WAITS AND BOB DYLAN | COOL DETATCHMENT | **ANDRE** CONFIDENCE | **DUBUS** CARPENTRY | X-RAYS | **III** JOBS THAT AREN'T IN RESTAURANTS | HOW DO YOU KNOW WHAT YOU KNOW? | WHAT HAUNTS US

Andre Dubus III

Springsteen, Tom Waits and Bob Dylan, How Do You Know What You Know?, What Haunts Us, X-Rays, Carpentry and Confidence, Cool Detachment, Jobs That Aren't in Restaurants

Andre Dubus III is the author of *House of Sand and Fog*, *Bluesman*, *The Garden of Last Days*, and *The Cage Keeper and Other Stories. The House of Sand and Fog* was an Oprah's Book Club selection and a finalist for the National Book Award. He lives with his family north of Boston.

Who are your major influences literary and otherwise?

Such a tough question. I don't know. It's hard to trace. It's like trying to figure out why you love somebody or how you came to say wouldn't instead of wasn't. It's really complex. I will tell you what comes to my mind, though. I'm the son of a great writer with the same name, but the truth is I didn't grow up thinking about writing. My mom and dad divorced when I was young. We had books in the house, but mom was a social worker and we lived in some poorer areas in the northeast. So I didn't think about literature a lot. Here's the thing, when I started writing about age 20-21, much to my surprise, I actually fell in love with a girl who was writing and I started to read her fiction and I got inspired. I hadn't read fiction since high school. Most of college I studied political science, sociology, and economics. I was really into the social sciences. And I just loved it, and I remember feeling really inspired when I put down just a student manuscript. It was a very good one, but I wanted to write a scene and that surprised me. Anyway, I came across this writer named, Breece D'J Pancake. His stories came out in the early '80s. He's from West Virginia and wrote beautifully about that part of the world; the hollows and the mine country and all the people who lived there. And I just felt so fed by his stories. Looking back now I realize how compassionate a writer he was, very generous and nonjudgmental towards his characters. His language was very sensual, stripped down and poetic. So that got my heart beating in a big way, but I have to say it was music. He was the literary influence that got me sparked, but Springsteen and Tom Waits and Bob Dylan. When I was a kid, at 15, I had every single Bob Dylan album. I've always liked songwriters who are literary.

You majored in Sociology at UT-Austin, and were accepted into a program in Marxist Studies at UW-Madison. Do you feel like a lot of your writing is somehow a response to problems you perceive in our society and the world at large?

I hope not. I tell you why. It's not an original thought, but I think that if your try to say something too political or philosophical in your fiction you run a good chance of killing it, unless you're a great, great writer, which I'm not. I think that, for me, the fiction that has fallen on its face is the fiction where I've tried to say something profound.

It's just fallen on its face. The fiction that works, whatever that means, are the ones where I went into them with more curiosity and passion to know what this experience might be like for another human being.

That interest that you talked about when I was younger had everything to do with hating bullying and bad behavior. I went to 14 schools before I got out of high school. I was always the new kid and I was a little kid. And I got picked on and beat up, actually a lot. In college I didn't see that my hatred for bullies, physical bullies, went to America foreign policy and Imperialism, which is the bully of the world as far as I'm concerned. I think we're still the bully of the world. I was just so angry, and I was at the University of Texas in Austin surrounded by 55,000 business majors who just want to go make a bunch of money and *fuck* the brown people and the earth, and I was just so angry. So I was going to go get a PhD.—the root was knowledge—I was going to get a PhD. then go to law school, and I thought I was going to be running for office. You know, a white liberal from Massachusetts. (laughter) They don't do so well, though. Do they? And then I fell in love with that girl and I started writing.

I think it's all unconscious. When I look at *House of Sand and Fog* I see a lot of political statement and some real overt themes, but I try not to be conscious of them when I work with them. I think Spike Lee is a really gifted guy, but I think some of his earlier films are so hamstrung by his trying to politicize them too much. You know, you have the guy who's the Malcolm X with the microphone, the Martin Luther King microphone, the white-cracker racist microphone guy. And I just feel that he is a marionette for the puppets. So, I try not to do that, that's all, but you never know how this stuff will come out. There's a great line from Flannery O'Connor's essay, "The Nature and Aim of Fiction." If you have to read one essay about writing, I would have students read that. One of the things she says is that a writer's beliefs are not what he sees but the light by which he sees. So you're still going to have this shit come up.

Since you're quoting O'Connor here, we will follow suit. O'Connor once said, "You don't dream up form and put truth in it. The truth creates its own form. Form is necessity in a work of art." How do you see this applying to your own work?

Well, first let me tell you, I love the Faulkner line, that the writer aspires to art. You know, my wife is a dancer and we're surrounded by people in the arts, but very few of my friends call themselves artists, and I don't call myself an artist either. I think it's for someone else to do. It's like you shouldn't call yourself a good lover, I mean how do you know? (laughter) I try to write art, but I don't know that I ever have, so already I have to qualify that to answer the question about necessity of *art*. I can tell you that my own way of struggling through this craft we all do is I prefer not to know what I'm doing. I always tell my writing students not to outline their stories and not to think about them, just to trust each line to take you to the deeper regions of where the story has to go, not even where you want to go. The writer doesn't get that choice. Often times I find structure as I go. I will find form and if it works it is because it is capturing some larger truth about the characters or their landscape or some theme I'm not even aware of. It's so intuitive. I know a lot of writers are very conscious of what they do and I am not, and the more conscious I get, the worse my writing gets. Not to say that I'm not really conscious once I redraft them—when I redraft them I work like a doctor looking at x-rays. But the form part is so intuitive. If it resonates in my gut that it works, I trust it's going to lead to another piece, which will show its own form. Does that make any sense? I think she's right on. I think it is all about truth.

Another quote from Flannery—because we like her so much—that caught when I was reading your stuff is something she said about violence. She said, "I suppose the reasons for the use of so much violence in modern fiction will differ with each writer who uses it, but in my own stories I have found that violence is strangely capable of returning my characters to reality and preparing them to accept their moment of grace." How do you think violence functions in your work and what do you see it accomplishing?

I've been interviewed so much in the last five years and I've never been asked that question, ever. Well...you know, here's the thing, you guys, there's a great line, well, the line everybody talks about, Sarah Orne Jewett, "write what you know," but I like E.L. Doctorow's line better, he said, "Yeah, but how do you know what you know?" (smiles) Isn't that great? How do you know what you know? If you think, well I'm a white, middle class kid who grew up in a condo, I can write about taking out the trash (laughter). How do you know what you know? There is more to your life than the literal facts of it.

I've had a lot of violence in my life, actually. I told you I was the new kid in town, so fist-fighting was the thing. I became a boxer in my early twenties and I fought my way out of this belief that I was this outside soft guy who should be beat up—that was driven into me as a kid all the time. I've lived in tough neighborhoods where violence was just normal. But you know I don't think about violence, I'm thinking now, you're right I got a lot of violence in my work (laughter). You know I've never even thought of that. There is a lot of violence in my work. This is an insight for me. How would I not know? In every story somebody gets raped, killed, shot, or beat up (continuous laughter). In *Bluesman*, my first novel, there's all sorts of death and destruction, *House of Sand and Fog*, is over-the-top worst-case-scenario.

I do think that we write about what haunts us. You guys fathers, yet?

No.

I wish it on you when it happens. It's such an experience. I'm blessed with three kids, two sons and a daughter. (Deep sigh) One of the things I know that I love about writing is in that line from Grace Paley, "We write what we don't know we know." It's an act of discovery and it's unfolding. I've learned a lot about my own demons, especially with *House of Sand and Fog*. I've read what people have written about it and I hear people talk about it and it's a blessing to get a reaction, at all, and I think, that is just where my fears are. I am haunted by how wrongly things can go in this world and the happier I am—and I'm in a very blessed time of my life with a strong marriage and beautiful kids and creativity and everything else—I can't sleep at night. My wife is a believer in Jesus Christ and God and I am not, yet I pray every day trying to get some belief, because I don't have enough faith. I really think that if I am not there to take care of business then everything is going to go to hell. It's just all these little boy fears that come out in these stories where it just all goes to hell. So, good, huh? Beats me. I don't even know if my answer is in there.

You've written while working in the academic world—teaching at Emerson, Tufts, Harvard—and you've written while working in the blue-

collar world—bartender, corrections officer, carpenter, bounty hunter—how do the two ends of the spectrum affect your writing and which type of job do you feel is more conducive to writing for you?

My publicist put out this wrong information on me and I keep having to fix it. You know, "he started writing later and he had all these jobs, then he started writing"—no. I took all those jobs because I started writing at about age 21, and they were night jobs and I like to write in the morning right after waking up. You guys like to write in the morning?

Night. Post-11:00 p.m.

Post 11:00? (laughs) Cool. Post 11:00. Well, this may be actually true for you, too, Edna O'Brien said she likes to go straight from sleep to the desk because she goes that way from the big room to the big room—from the dream world of the subconscious to the dream world of the writing. I think when you're up that late you're in the dream world anyways. Richard Bausch had a great line. He said, "if you think you are thinking when you are writing then think again, because you are much closer to that dream state you get into when you're day-dreaming and dreaming."

The bartending and the private investigating I did for six months in my early twenties. I actually went to Mexico looking for a killer, if you can believe that, and I've never written a word about it either.

Let me answer your question. The physical blue-collar jobs I worked until I was about 30. I didn't know that you could have a job where you didn't break a sweat. I didn't know that. I always worked hard bartending or banging nails or being a short order cook. I didn't know that you could actually have jobs where you could sit down and not break a sweat and I had this blue-collar distrust—that's not work, come on, go hang some five-eighths sheetrock overhead, buddy. That's work (laughter). And then I started teaching and I'd come home shit-assed exhausted from just talking.

Which one's better? From carpentry, this is what I have learned. I was a bad carpenter when I began. It's such a tough thing to be good at and I've finally gotten to be a good carpenter after 18 years at it. Carpentry gave me confidence. It takes balls, chutzpah, ovaries, whatever you want to call it. You walk into a room and they say, "You know we have an office here and we'd like to take the wall out, put a room up there, and put a bathroom there were the living room is and a kitchen there." And you say, "Okay." And then when you actually do it, you really feel a sense of confidence pervade your body. I thought if I can build a bathroom where there once stood a deck, I can write a chapter, can't I? That's how that affected that.

The bartending was really great because I got to be an eavesdropper. You know how bartenders are; if you're sitting at the bar and the bartender is wiping down tables, it's amazing, the bartender will be three inches away wiping down your ash tray and you'll be saying, "I just don't think I love you, and I never did, and I'm going out with Harry." You just forget he's even there. I would hear all sorts of stuff and I enjoyed that. And again I liked the late hours and having cash in my pocket and then waking up and going right to writing.

Teaching has taught me more than anything though. Sophocles once said, "If you want to learn, teach." I learn so much from my writing students' triumphs and their failures. For years I taught these writing workshops and I mistakenly believed that when it was your turn in the hot seat that that was when you were going to learn, actually that's when you are going to learn the least. You're going to learn that you hate being in the hot seat. You're going to learn the most criticizing other people's work, because you're not married to it and that's where you can really hone those critical skills.

So I would say all of the above. The one that's best, I don't know. I think if the teaching is not too much—at one time during the composition of *House Of Sand And Fog* I was teaching at five campuses, and remodeling two houses. Sleeping four hours a night and writing in my car—that was not good. I think two courses a semester is plenty, after that you start to get this midwife syndrome, where you're helping everyone else have a baby, but you're not having your own. I would say a job that does not deplete you physically and does not deplete you too much mentally is ideal. So basically, you know, a part time job.

Any good jokes from your days tending bar?

Yeah, I got one. It's my favorite.

This Irish guy walks into the bar. He says, (clears his throat to pull out his best Irish accent) "Hey bartender, give me three pints, please."

The bartender says, "Three pints, you're just one guy, what do you want three pints for?"

"Well, I've got two brothers back in Ireland and I always have one for them."

"Oh that's nice, I have brothers too." So he pours him the three pints of Guinness. This Irish guy comes back every night for the next six months and orders three pints of beer. One night he comes in and says, "Yeah, yeah, bartender, just give me two pints."

"Oh no, bud, don't tell me, bad news at home."

"Oh, no, no, nothing like that. I just gave up drinking."

House of Sand and Fog *was somewhat painful to read, because the characters are on this downward spiral from page one until the end. How painful was it to write, if at all?*

Well, Capote had a great line. He said, the job of the writer is to write as cool and detached as a surgeon. And I used to hate that line, cause I thought, yeah you can be cool and detached Truman, but I'm a passionate French/Irishman, buddy. No cool detachment from me, but I was wrong and he was right, of course. I actually began to think more about that line after seeing literal surgery. My wife had three C-sections for our kids and I was in on a C-section before that—my father's third wife. I was in the operating room when she had the baby, because he was in his wheelchair he couldn't sit where the husband sits, so I sat with her. We were the same age and she was like a pal of mine and when they opened her up—they take this big scalpel and put their hands in there—and I felt nothing. I said, huh, I got a stomach for this. Chekhov was a writer and a doctor. I could be a surgeon and a writer. I was just thinking I missed my calling, yeah right. And then it's time for my wife to get a C-section and I'm about to throw up. (Whiny voice) 'Oh, don't cut my wife open, that's my wife. That's my baby!'

I say all this because writing the book, even in the hardest scenes, even in the fateful scenes with the child—I felt nothing. Just scalpel, sponge, sutures. I was just trying my best, which I always feel is not enough, just trying to write as truly to the story as I can without steering it any way with what I want to happen. That said though, I'm a little full of shit. Truth is, I felt this kind of cloud over me the whole time writing it. There'd be this cloud as I began to sit down and I'd have to work through it, then I'd have to run five miles, or drink or do something to relieve myself to get out of that energy. The irony is that while I was writing it, I was going through one of the most joyous times of my life. We were having three kids while I was writing that. It's strange isn't it? All that darkness coming out.

Fate seems to be a major element present in House Of Sand And Fog. *It also seems to participate in the naturalist tradition, along the lines of Dreiser and Norris. How did you go about the construction of this novel, and did you have any other novels in mind while writing it?*

Yeah, but it was subconscious. I didn't know. One of the reasons I think it's important for writers to read a lot is not so you can steal actual lines, because that's plagiarism, but you can steal structure. You can learn so much. Right now, Patricia Henley is reading Alice Munro's new book and we were talking about how much we love her and she said, reading her, she feels like she's her literary mother because she says 'oh, you can do that, and you can do that,' you know, where these writers break rules and boundaries and give you new freedom. That summer before I started writing that novel [*House of Sand and Fog*] I had just finished reading Richard Price's *Clockers*, which is a bad Spike Lee movie, but it's a damn good book. He's a really good writer from New York. And I didn't even know this until I did an interview in Germany for the German edition of *House of Sand and Fog*, which is called House of Sand and *Naandegescherheimen*. (laughter) That was a whole bizarre experience. That book is in languages I don't even know what they are. Anyway, a German interview asked me that same question and I said it was *Clockers*, because it was told from the point of view of two voices marching side-by-side, completely different. One was a fourteen-year-old black, street kid named Strike, who deals crack, and the beauty of this literary form is that you quickly love him. A crack dealer, who deals crack to kids, you root for him. I love how that happens. And the other voice is this middle aged, dumpy, Jewish homicide detective, who's in a bad marriage and hunting Strike. And I didn't consciously think, gee, I'd like to try this sometime. But I know now, looking back, if I hadn't read *Clockers* before writing this [*House of Sand and Fog*] I wouldn't have even thought it possible. I somehow was given implicit permission to have the two voices marching side-by-side.

This kind of goes along with what you just were talking about. It's the Lester question. We didn't expect him to come in all of a sudden part two and then in the third person, also. I was wondering if you had any idea of where that decision came from. The duel first person makes it easy to get the reader involved. Did you ever toy around with trying an omniscient voice at all?

I did. Did that third person, when it went to part two and sort of a more authorial third person with limited omniscience, did that jar you? Or did that not work for you?

It was a surprise, obviously. I was surprised that Lester got that much attention because it seemed to be so much about Kathy and the Col.

Here's the thing, Beckett had this great line, and I love it and I hate it, though. It's encouraging and discouraging all at once, but here it goes, he said, "Ever try, ever failed, never mind. Try again, fail better." Isn't that great—fucking Irish. It punches and kisses you all at the same time. What I'm saying is, the book has a lot of success and I'm grateful. It's a wonderful thing, but I'm haunted by it like everything else I've ever wrote and one of the things I would change is I would incorporate Lester's voice earlier. I do feel it comes a little late and it's a little bit jolty. 'Okay, I get it now, why he is the way that he is.' I think it should have been a bit more organic, but I'll stand by it because the flaws in a work are also part of its own artistry. You have to live with them and move on and except it. To answer your question about omniscient voice—I did try all sorts of voices, all the time, to see which would fit. But listen to this—this is kind of mysterious and "Ooooooo," Ouija board. I started the Colonel first and it took me days and weeks to get a feel for his voice—I tried first person present, past; second person—that's a cool one; third person present, I liked that one a lot but it wasn't working. He only started having a sound in first person present. Then with Kathy I tried all these different sounds and she only revealed herself in first person past. Lester, when I got to him, when I got to that white space where Kathy is in the house I knew I had to go to him, But I still think I should restructure that book, anyway, I tried first person and he sounded like a cartoon character cowboy, (big Texas voice) "Well, I'm waiting for my woman here on the porch. Where's my woman? Where's my gun?" It sounded bad. So he only came in this more omniscient voice. But here's the Ouija board thing—and all this is intuitive, it's all just gut stuff cause I didn't know how the story was going to end, I certainly wasn't trying to write a tragedy, matter of fact I didn't think of it as a tragedy in the dramaturgical sense until reviewers referred to it that way—isn't it bizarre that the character who doesn't survive the story is in present tense? He's the only one who could have been in present tense. Ooooooooooo. I love it.

A lot of us MFA students here at Purdue wanted Kathy Nicolo's blood to be spilled. What made you decide to keep her alive?

I like your word choice because I do try in my work not to decide anything. I want to explain myself. I read a very articulate review in some big paper, which I've repressed because it was so bad (laughter). No the writer had some good things to say about the book, but the writer said, (snobby, high-pitched voice) "Where are you Mr. Dubus? Where are you? How am I supposed to interpret this?" At first, for a couple of days, I thought, he's right, damn it. A real writer would have been more in the book and would have directed and guided more and then I thought, screw that. I like books where I feel lost, like the writer has abandoned me like a bad mother and it's just up to me and my dark streets to work through. The truth is, I try not to ever decide anything. I try to find the true moment and write the next true moment and rewrite any moment that isn't true to the piece, and I realized over the years that if you do that you end up saying something universal that you didn't know you were trying to say or you didn't know was in you. A friend of mind said the same thing. He said, man, you kept the wrong person alive at the end. I hated her. And I said, Well, that's just...I...that's just how it went. I didn't choose. I empathize with that response, but it was out of my hands.

What do you think about this current explosion of writing programs? What do you think are the biggest advantage of being in one, and what is the biggest danger of being in one?

Oh boy. Sometimes I'm employed in these writing programs and sometimes I'm not. I'm not in an MFA program now as a teacher, but I have taught MFA programs in the past. Part of me thinks it's a racket.

There are a few too many of them and I wonder if it's not just a way to give writers jobs that aren't in restaurants. Part of me thinks that. But I'd say only 10 percent of me thinks that. 90 percent of me is less cynical.

Let me state the negative first and then I'll get to the more hopeful. I've visited a lot of programs, I've been to a lot of conferences, and I've heard a lot of horror stories. I think there are a lot of good writers out there who are bad writing teachers. Just because somebody can write a good book doesn't mean they can teach you how to write a good book. I think that teaching is a real calling and that it takes a certain kind of sensibility and not everybody has got it. Conversely, you can have great writing teachers who aren't such good writers themselves. It doesn't matter. My wish is that more programs have better teachers in them, and I don't care how their publishing is going or how their writing is going. I think that a lot of teaching is just overly destructive in MFA programs. I think there is a lot of political stuff going on. There is a star system where the talented ones get singled out and ones who don't show immediate talent, which is, how do you know? Get kind of left behind. All of that I rail against and don't like.

I believe that if you have a good writing teacher—and let me define that, I think a good writing teacher is not one who is imposing his or her writing style or preferences on you, but is simply trying to listen to your muse and is trying to guide you to your own best work as it presents itself to the teacher. I think of the Hemingway line, that every writer needs a built-in, shock-proof shit detector, and I think that the job of the good writing teacher is simply to hone and to strengthen and embolden your shit detector. Activate that shit detector, so that when you're off alone for years with nobody reading your work and nobody giving a shit, you know how to cut all that you should cut out of your work.

You know, I'm unusual, I had a really good writer for a parent and even through divorce, when I didn't live with him, I still knew a writer. Porter Shreve, who I've just met and I really like, his mom is a writer. I'm sure your parents aren't writers, right? Most parents are dairy farmers or dentists or housewives. The culture, it's fascinating, the culture will elevate you and celebrate you once you've had some commercial success with your art, but they will tell your whole life not to do it because you can't make a living. They will discourage you in every way possible. And parents, I can understand why they do it. Here's the really big thing that writing programs give writers who don't know writers—and most don't: a sense of community. A sense that you're not just this weird little guy doing this weird little thing in the closet like a bad habit. It's really a noble calling and I think you'll make friendships in the MFA program that will last a lifetime. Because if you just have that one person you can count on to be honest with your work or that one person you can call at three o'clock in the morning to bitch and moan with, that's a real blessing. If that's all you get out of a MFA program I think it's worth the money. I really do.

What are you working on these days?

I could tell you, but I'd have to kill you. I can never talk about a work in progress. It's like masturbating before you make love. When you are writing a story you are pregnant with the story and you have to protect it until it's ready to come out. I can tell you this: I'm working on a novel.

What advice do you have for the unpublished writers sweating out there?

Don't think about the world ever noticing or caring about what you write. Write because if you don't write you're simply not you. When I started writing I felt like myself for the first time. Make a living and steal your writing time. I know how sweet it is to be published, but I know about rejection too. I've had three yes's and 117 no's over the past six years. *The Cage Keeper* went through 29 publishers, *Bluesman* 18, *House Of Sand And Fog* 24. Honestly, if I had a divine premonition that I would never be published again I would still write. It's a better day to have written badly than to not have written at all. If you're writing four, five or six days a week because you can't help yourself, the world is eventually going to take notice.

2005

ABOUT THE INTERVIEWERS: **Barney T. Haney** is the assistant manager of a small state university farm in Lake Charles, Louisiana, where he teaches inmates and students about agriculture, among his many other duties. Currently he's writing a novel centered around commercial salmon fishing in Bristol Bay. At the time of the interview, he was managing editor of *Sycamore Review.* **Patrick Kelly** earned his MFA in fiction in 2005. He was the fiction editor of *Sycamore Review* at the time of the interview.

FISTFIGHTS | RACE IN THE SOUTH | CHILDREN ON THE EDGE | **RICHARD** WOMANIZING | **FORD** WILDCARDS | THANKLESS, USELESS, LAZY BUMS

Richard Ford

Fistfights and Boxing, Wildcards, Race in the South, Children on the Edge, Womanizing, Thankless, Useless, Lazy Bums

Richard Ford was born in Jackson, Mississippi, in 1944. He has published five novels and three collections of stories, including *The Sportswriter, Independence Day, Wildlife, A Multitude of Sins* and *The Lay of the Land. Independence Day* was awarded the Pulitzer Prize and the PEN/Faulkner Award for Fiction.

It occurred to me that many of your stories seem to start where other people's tend to end. Often, a lot of the "action" has already taken place and the characters seem engaged in some process of coming to terms. Is this a conscious starting-point, and, if it is, what is it about this state or condition that interests you the most?

That's an interesting prospect even if it's not true. I never felt that about my stories. I think I like what I find to be most dramatic and original, which is to say the things that ordinary life might overlook or that human beings may not be sensitive to or take seriously. That's what I think I write about. But putting it in the frame in which you cast it, I am interested in the consequence of acts. It's not so much that I think that death, or the diminution of passion, or someone's going off to Montana for the rest of their life isn't interesting. But what intrigues me the most is how those acts cause other subsequent actions. I'm sure there are plenty of other writers attracted to the same kinds of human drama as I am. For me, what fiction is often about is the way in which the past impends upon the present and somehow prefigures the future. Morality, that is to say our notion of what is good and what is bad, is always bound up in how we entertain and adapt to the consequences that lodge in the dramas.

I was first introduced to your work in Matters of Life and Death, *a collection edited by Tobias Wolff. In the introduction he says "The works in this collection remind us that our house is built on sand and the stories represent what it means to be human."*

A biblical reference from Toby. A practicing Christian against all odds.

What are those moments that you obsess about when you consider a house built on sand?

Well, I don't obsess about anything, except sometimes about whether I have cancer. But what I think a house built on sand might refer to is all of those contingent things in our lives which we may take for granted or not notice precisely. Who loves us and who we love. Where we live, and how long can we live there. How are we able to find a vocation and keep it. But, probably of all those three, the most poignant to me, the most important, is who do we love and who loves us and how long will it last? How are we able, in the congeries, the rough-and-tumble of life, to go on defining love and affection among the things we know? Or, if you don't like love, sympathy. Or, just how are we able to reimagine and reinvent life so that we will enjoy it more? Or at least live it tolerably? The nature of modern life—and you could say this throughout centuries—is that we are constantly being bombarded with various kinds of doubts which probably cause us not to believe what we would like to firmly believe. This is the grains of sand part, I guess. Doubt and its consequences upon our lives. And what we try to do is erect firmer pillars than the first time we erected them. We try to do better. It's one of the moral elements in fiction: people trying to do better. Often they fail. But the story has a moral element because it shows them trying and because it concerns itself with such issues at all.

You mention modern life, which is exactly the phrase Austin uses over the phone when his wife questions who the woman is who he had dinner with. His explanation is "la vie modern." *Would you agree that Austin is being bombarded by the kind of doubt you just mentioned?*

Contingency. George Will said—not that he's a great sage, but he is a pretty smart guy, his politics not withstanding—he said the reason to study history is to learn how to deal with contingency. I think one of the reasons to read literature is to learn how to deal with contingency. Contingency is the kind of cancerous doubt that insinuates itself into all kinds of modern existence. But, it always has. You can read it in Chaucer. You can read it in "the Wife of Bath's Tale." By modern I don't mean contemporary, but life that anybody's lived since the Dark Ages.

You've touched on the idea of history a few times. When I was reading through your work, I was thinking of your movement from the private, personal histories explored in Rock Springs *to the more communal or national type of history that shows up in* Independence Day. *How do you see the relationship between public and private histories operating in your fiction?*

Well, it is a conscious movement, but I don't think of it at all as a progress. It may represent an oscillation from something more private, as you say, to something more public, to what Emerson calls "municipal virtues." There's an old saw which says, "All politics is local'" and I think that all politics is really personal, that all larger political issues just bear dramas that exist in our lives on rather small personal bases. Insofar as *Independence Day* does address in a more public way those municipal virtues, it's just my attempt to try to show another dimension to what might have been just personal in *Rock Springs* or in *Wildlife.* It's just my attempt to say, look. in fact, if you set a story in New Jersey in an election year, there are just the same kinds of things that people were suffering and experiencing elsewhere in Great Falls, Montana: loss of love, disenchantment, disengagement, contingency, the provisional nature of looking to the future. When you set those stories over here and put them in a political context, they make the same kind of sense.

You talk about the idea of oscillation rather than progress.

Well, I'm trying to do better as a writer. Although when I finished writing "Occidentals" in 1996, I just put my head in my hands and said, "My God, what's wrong with you? What made you write a story like that?"

I would like to try to tie this into you as a writer in terms of developing character. I've read that you're interested in "the incalculability of life."

Yeah, that's Forester's term in *Aspects of The Novel.*

Is it within the realm of human possibility to see a character like Earl from "Rock Springs" potentially develop into a character like Frank Bascombe or Austin or Charley Matthews?

If you do an arcing line from Earl, could you ever find that line touching back down on Frank or Charley or Austin?

Yes.

I really don't know. But people have said to me that because of the way the little boy narrator in "Jealous" starts his life, it was feasible to think that he could end up like Charley in "Occidentals." Well, that's interesting, but I would never have said that, only because it seemed to me to lack inevitability. Since you started out talking about human possibility, accidents intervene in so many people's lives, lives are so unpredictable, so provisional, that it seems to me that a kid like the narrator of "Jealous" could end up in any variety of ways. One of them might be Charley Matthews, but because there are so many other possibilities, I wouldn't want to say that it was inevitable. If you believe in the redemptive possibilities in life then inevitability is the thing you are fundamentally at war with. And I do believe that.

Mary Gordon wrote, "Destiny, fatedness, is the great bugaboo of American literature." I didn't understand what that meant for a long time. But in a way, I understand what she means. It refers to the war we wage to exert our will over contingency and possibility and accident and all the things that might betray us. So for the boy who narrates "Jealous," I would hope that good could come of his life, that he could take this experience that he has with his aunt and make good out of it. I wouldn't want to sell him short. So it wouldn't seem to mean he would necessarily become like Charley Matthews in "Occidentals," though of course it could. Just like I could end up on the street someday. Though I hope I don't.

Some of the stories in Rock Springs *focus on children, with the adults living their lives in the background.* The Sportswriter *and* Independence Day *seem to reverse this. I was wondering what you saw as the connection between the adults and the children in your fiction.*

Apart from the most obvious ones, probably not very much. I like to have kids in stories because they're the wild cards. You can fashion kids to make them probably no more precocious nor valuable than kids really are in life, or you can make them little Greek choruses on the goings on in the foreground, on what the adults are doing. I'm principally interested in adults, though, And insofar as kids are in the stories at all, their importance draws upon their likelihood to become adults. I'm not very interested in their little underdeveloped lives and minds. I'm interested in the way in which they vector toward adults and judge what adults do and comment on adult life. But the drama of their lives is, how will they become affirmable adults?

I find that Cherry from "Sweethearts" is a character who a reader can worry about and question how she will ever become an affirmable adult, especially within the tough world where she lives.

Cherry has a father who loves her, though.

Yes, she does.

And Arlene in that story is a pretty strong, self-directed woman. I would think that Cheryl in "Rock Springs" maybe has an even dicier future. I think that's something I'm always interested in—children on the edge, children whose futures are slightly jeopardized by the violent, insufficiently caring acts of adults. I prefer a story to focus your attentions and sentiments on the adults. What you should say to yourself is, "What's going to happen to this little girl?" As soon as you ask that, the lens opens a little wider and you see the context. Then the questions are, what can these adults do to act responsibly, and what can they do to look out for her future? For me, to write just about a child in jeopardy wouldn't be enough.

In The Sportswriter *and* Independence Day, *one of the things I liked were the "kid's jokes." In* Independence Day, *for example, Paul tells his father, "A horse comes into a bar and orders a beer." and the bartender says, "Gee, why the long face?"*

He told all the bad jokes that I knew.

The small little jokes do reveal something about the nature of Frank and his son's relationship. It shows them communicating through a very innocent type of language.

The jokes are there just mostly to amuse me and the reader, and to make Paul seem less demonic. And they're there for reasons humor is often there, to relieve you from some of the heavy-going which occurs in the story. I just think if nothing's funny, nothing's serious. Humor shines a new light on the serious. It's nothing new, really.

You said in an interview with Paris Review *that a lot of your humor grew out of the absurdity of the racist society in which you were raised. I was wondering if it comes from anything other than an outgrowth of absurdity.*

My mother and father were laughers. They liked to laugh. My mother grew up and somehow knew a lot about burlesque. My mother loved burlesque humor. My parents both loved broad bodily humor. Slapstick. They liked things to be unsubtly funny, and so do I. I've been told many times that I have the sense of humor of a fourth-grader, and that's fine with me because at least I've got a sense of humor at all. I'm not sitting around with a long face. And I don't think it's a stretch to say that the racial situation in the South created a sense of banal absurdity for all of us white kids. There was a sense I had that we weren't even really living a life. As long as we were sort of prevented from dealing with all those other people who lived on the other side of town, how do we have any claim to full reality? It made the ether we breathed to be very thin and rare because we weren't living fully, and it made absurdity almost inevitable.

But then there was that other side, too. My grandmother and my grandfather were just rough-and-tumble people who grew up on the railroad. My grandfather was a professional boxer. They just were rough people. Their kind don't even exist today. They had a real low, sometimes lewd, sometimes vituperative humor. They made fun of people. They were happy to somehow escape the poverty of the Ozarks where they grew up and get someplace better.

It's interesting that you chose to have Paul tell the more harmless jokes rather than the "rough-and-tumble" ones since, at least in Independence Day, *he appears to be somewhat disturbed.*

Well, there are certain jokes that you can't persuasively put in a little boy's mouth. There are a lot of jokes that you just wouldn't have him tell, so you do have to suit the joke to the fact that he's fifteen years old, while not trying to make him typical, because he isn't typical—he's a character in a book after all. So he's very atypical. But the kinds of jokes that fifteen-year-old boys tell are jokes that I still find funny. And you're right, they're mostly harmless, jokes about animals and word-play jokes, things like that.

They're fun, too.

They mean to be. If they're not fun when you read them, it doesn't matter what they connect to. From *The Sportswriter,* you know, "Who's Irish and lives in your back yard? Paddy O'Furniture." I still think that's very funny.

I really enjoyed your essay "In the Face," republished in The Best American Essays 1997, *chronicling the number of fist fights you've had in your life.*

Good. Did you think I was going to be a bad guy?

It startled me.

Yes, it's startling.

It struck me as a deeply personal essay. I was wondering what compelled you to write it and if you have any reservations about revealing so much about yourself.

I did have reservations about it. What compelled me to write it was that I said I would write an essay about boxing, and I knew a lot about boxing. And yet the kinds of straightforward, Leiblingesque boxing essays that I might have thought I wanted to write, when the time came, just weren't available to me, or I didn't have an interest in them. I sort of got beached on the problem of writing a more standard essay. Then I just sort of worked from that and asked, "What's possible here? What could I possibly write that could be remotely about boxing?"

I had boxed and my grandfather was a boxer. And I thought maybe there were some things out of that era of my life that I could use. I had been in a few fights in my life. I've done some bad things, some humiliating things, and had some bad things done to me. And I thought, well here you go.

I didn't like telling the story about kissing a guy's butt who threatened to kick the shit out of me in a public street. But then I thought, I've been carrying this story around with me a long time, basically shrinking away from it like a ninny. So maybe that's what this essay's for, to get that off my mind. I hadn't thought about it for a long time.

Nobody who gets into fights isn't scared to death, and I've been scared a lot of times.

You also reveal the impulse to hit as something that's a part of your "deep memory," something hardwired into you as a child when your grandfather taught you how to fight. Can anything take on that same status now?

You mean take on the same status as the will to strike out at someone when I finally don't understand him and he threatens me?

Yes, something that you learned when you were very young but never questioned until much later.

I have an impulse, which is pretty hard-won, to take responsibility for things. If something bad happens, it's my standard impulse to say it's not your fault, it's my fault. And I don't mean to say that in a self-sacrificing guilty way. I just try to find a vocabulary for assuming responsibility for acts. It causes me to internalize a lot of responsibility and sometimes feel grief about it, taking responsibility for things which I'm not responsible for but would like to try to be to make life seem more rational.

Is that more of a learned lesson, or do you think that was instilled in you the way the hitting was?

I don't know enough about human origins to know that. I was an only child. I didn't have anybody obvious to blame for the stuff I did. All I could do was lie about it whether I did it or not. And I did plenty of that. I got caught at so many things because I was the only child. If it was done and I was around, I did it. So I guess I learned early on to face the consequences.

I'm curious about the idea of internalizing responsibility. In the final paragraph of "Rock Springs," Earl begins to question the person he sees in the window as "you." Not only is Earl, as the first person narrator, asking the reader what judgment he or she has made of Earl's character, but it's almost as if you as the writer are questioning the reader. The reader is then forced to take responsibility.

That's right. That's what I intended.

Is internalizing responsibility something that is important in your fiction?

Well. I think it is important for people like Earl. It's a gesture from Earl to the world in which he says, "Aren't we really alike? If you look down on me from that window and you see me looking in this window, you might think that I was stealing something, getting ready to steal this car, or doing something shady. But in fact, here I'm just doing what you're doing up there in your own window. Isn't it that we're alike?"

Just as with the end of *Independence Day,* I think that a sense of shared impulse, a sense of sharing the planet together, is a very important experience to have. I'm like you. You're like me. We are not alone. I suppose it does make the unseen person in the window share a responsibility of being like Earl.

I don't like, and I never have liked, a sense of elitism. I don't like the impulse that people have to exclude others. I saw its damaging effects when I was young. I think in a way, being a writer is a little bit of a response to seeing the malignant consequences of exclusion. Writers join people with their work.

That reminds me of "In the Face." One reason you said you didn't find hitting particularly interesting was that there was no optimism attached to it.

Right. Little good comes of it.

Is the idea of optimism all impulse that drives much of your fiction?

Yes. I think if loneliness is the disease, the story is the cure. Trying to write stories, which you do for other people, is a gesture of trying to make something good in the world, for the world to be better.

You have a belief in the sentiment contained in the question, "What are reading and writing stories for if not to make us better people?"

I certainly subscribe to it. You can read it in Camus if you want to in his long essay called "The Situation of the Writer in 1947," or in his essay "Why Write?"

In The Sportswriter, *Frank has a line, "There is no hope unless we can forget and forgive the past." What role do you think memory has in your fiction. And are the stories you write your ways of forgiving?*

Yes. I suppose so. When you have a story like those first person narrations in *Rock Springs*, or a story like *Wildlife* or "Jealous," the moral structure of the story is, I will tell you what happened to me as a way of ordering it, giving it a sense of logic, demonstrating my dominion over it at this point in my life, so that once it's ordered and set in this particular structure and made tidy, I can go on. The end of "Optimists," when the boy's mother comes and kisses him, is, for me, the most poignant thing I ever wrote because it forgives and comprehends so much. It so much says, "Oh well, we did that. I want you to understand how you felt about things then, how they were and how it's all right."

A matter of remembering things you didn't even know you knew?

Well, at least putting the things you did know into an order which makes them seem livable, forgivable, and logical. If you look back at your past and all you see is a jumble of things which you don't understand, it can prejudice you against living a life of any consequence. When you come out of a chaos, are you then going into a world you hope is orderly enough to like?

To begin to order it through language.

Yeah. Language is the thing. That's why, in *Independence Day*, the words "locution, locution, locution" keep coming up. It's how you order the world in words.

You had mentioned that "Independence" was a word that triggered you into Independence Day. *Did you have any specific word or words which drove you into the novellas from* Women With Men*?*

"Translation" was the sort of motive word for me in "Occidentals." I wanted to call it "The Translator," but Ward Just had already written a book called *The Translator*. He's a friend of mine and I didn't want to step on his title. Again, it just has one of those qualities that words have for me sometimes, which is a kind of density. It seems to have, in a spatial way, something behind it, and I knew what it meant literally and what it meant in all its different uses. And I thought, well, is there some way in which I can write a story to consolidate all its uses and make them sensible and maybe even invent new sense?

In "Jealous," "jealous" was the word; that's why I called it that. I thought that all the characters in "Jealous" could be said to be typified by there being one person jealous of another. Doris is jealous of her sister. Doris is jealous of Larry. Larry's father is a little jealous of Larry. And so forth. Everybody has, in some way, that kind of relationship. And that's my view of looking at it before and after. It defines experience in a new way and extends the use of that word. Jealous.

With "The Womanizer," it was the idea of "womanize." It was a word I kept hearing around. I thought I'd write a story which investigated it, and the investigation turned out to be defining what I felt womanizers were, if they were anything at all: that is, people who never look outside themselves. Womanizing isn't necessarily behavior that describes having many relationships with many people, which is the way it is usually described. If you have a relationship into which you are not fully engaged and have the capacity to cause harm to another, then that's what it means to womanize. It means to turn another human being into a slightly unloved object. Even if you only do it once.

In "Occidentals," Charley Matthews seems to write a novel to help him deal with his failed marriage, and he also seems to write for revenge, painting an unflattering picture of his ex-wife. In a lot of ways, though, the book he's written hasn't helped him. He's still struggling. Does the book's failure compel him to go on and keep trying to order the world through language?

Not that writing stories is therapy. It isn't at all. Not for me anyway. But it is possible to assign values to certain issues when you write about them. And maybe by doing so you learn something about them so that you don't have to repeat the same problems. That's certainly one good that you hope a reader will take from a story. In a story, you see people acting in destructive ways, profligate ways and hope that the reader will say, "Gee, I hope that wouldn't happen to me. I see what the consequences of this kind of action are." That may be wishful thinking.

In my particular life it would be wishful thinking. I write about things and then go on and do them again.

You spoke earlier about writing for forgiveness. Have you, like Charley, ever written for something like revenge?

I don't think so. I don't usually write about real people. I don't ever make any gestures toward revenge. Once in a while I have written about someone I knew, but I don't think I ever did it for revenge.

I'm a kind of spontaneous person. If I feel the need to revenge myself, I do it directly. Normally, I don't brood or hold grudges. I have a bad enough temper, and the virtue of having a quick response is that it gets the problem out, it gets it over. Literature is too high a calling to make it the hand-servant of those low kinds of impulses.

I've read that there is no suitable word for someone who writes literature. We have music and the musician, art and the artist, but we don't necessarily have literature and the literaturist.

Well, just call us bums. Thankless, useless, lazy bums.

You've mentioned that, as a writer, you felt it was one of your jobs to narrow your reader's options as much as possible. I was wondering if there are ever any places in your fiction where you really wanted to open things up for interpretation.

No. I want to do the opposite. I will do all the opening for myself. That's one of the pleasures of being a writer. I can see the full display of possibility. James said the wonderful awful whole of art is free selection. And I do the selecting. I know what I want somebody to think about. I know it despite the fact that others will sometimes not agree with me, have a different view and think I failed at it. But do I want purposefully to leave things to the reader's interpretation? No. I want to open the aperture wider for the reader. But I determine what the final circumference of the aperture is. I want, for instance with independence—which most people define as typified by isolation—I want the readers of *Independence Day* to think, well, isolation is just one of its attributes. Another one is that when you're independent, you're free to make important liaisons with others. You act on independence by acting freely and touching others, reaching out and making contact and taking that risk. Independence is one of those qualities you have which empowers you to make those things. In one way, I want to open the aperture wider. But once you get it opened wider, then I want you to see what I want you to see.

I understand your point of wanting your reader to see what you want them to see, but in terms of developing a character, you mentioned in Paris Review *that you don't want them to fall into a trap that you predict for them since characters' reactions grow organically out of the scene. How do you balance the two?*

I don't know that you do balance it. You know the reader will always be on his or her own warrant. What I'm trying to do is be sure that among the many possibilities that a reader will think of and entertain, he or she will at least entertain all the ones I'm offering. And then whatever comes after that, in whatever way the reader wants to deviate from the track or stop at a particular moment and start again later and completely spoil my sense of the scenes' rhythms, I want the story that I understand to always be available. Cutting into a tree, I want the reader to see the same grains.

When you look at that grain in terms of character development, do you focus on the grand scheme, such as a character dealing with loss, or do you concentrate on the microelements like particular gestures and mannerisms?

I think the solution to that question can be shown through the situation in which, for instance, Frank is living the aftermath of his son's death. Well, that takes care of the grand scheme right there. But when one deals with loss, we deal with it in terms of which shoe we tie first. We deal with it in terms of what color suit we wear. We deal with it in terms of whether we have a bright word to say to our secretaries every morning. And that's what dealing with loss turns out to be. And that's the basic moral charge of realistic fiction: that inherent in those small gestures is a connection to larger issues, and we are better off if we take interest in those small gestures as a way of dealing with the large issues, as a way of reconciling ourselves to them, as a way of living life more efficiently and better.

There's a line in "The Womanizer" where Austin says that even realists need a break now and then. Austin is someone who perceives himself as a realist, yet he still role plays around his wife.

Absolutely.

Is realism more about resolving oneself to this type of condition more than facing things directly?

I think when Austin says that about himself he is *saying* that he is a realist. But what I think he *means* is, he's married. For Austin, realism is being married. You're joined with another person and you have to live reciprocally and that's what realism is. You go to your job and you meet your wife after work and you have a drink and you get a little twisted and you have an argument and maybe you leave. That's what realism is to *him*. In other words, it's the down side, at least it seems so at this moment in his life. It needn't always be the down side, of course. Yet what I would say about Austin is that he's in fact not very much of a realist. For him to be a persuasive realist, he would have to understand a little more about what he's doing with Josephine. He would have to understand that maybe, if he's a realist, going back to Paris is not the absolute best thing to do. As a matter of fact, he's living in a kind of dream world. If you say, "Austin, you don't have children. You don't like children. Don't get stuck here in this apartment with this child, and then take the child out into the Jardin du Luxembourg. Don't get to whirling away your hours wondering about your own future while this child is taken off to the bushes and molested." So he's not a realist. He's a solipsist.

I found myself cringing when Austin was in the park with the little boy.

Me too. I found it to be a very painful piece of writing. And there were people who didn't like it, who just thought it was just way too excessive. But I wanted it to be excessive because I wanted to show what the excessive consequences can be of self-infatuation, of living in a fantasy life.

We know something terrible happened to the boy in the woods, but you do leave enough room open to suggest that maybe something was started, but not finished.

I meant it to be that the boy was not raped. But he was molested. Maybe he wasn't penetrated. Maybe he wasn't made to do horrible things. But he was definitely taken out there and stripped. I've spent some time in the Jardin du Luxembourg, and believe me, all kinds of unthinkable things go on among those trees and bushes. Anybody in France who has read that story—it's not published in French—but anybody who has read it, knows.

In a short essay you wrote entitled "Sense of Place," you talked about language and the way it's applied to place, how people can connect through such representations about place. A couple of times in "Occidentals," Purdue itself was mentioned and it conjured up all sorts of things for me as I was reading it.

I'm not going to read that part tomorrow. I would probably get clubbed off the stage.

I wasn't sure if you had been here or not.

I've never been here. At least not physically.

How important is it for you to actually see a place you write about?

It's not important at all.

What's your sense of responsibility to a particular place?

None.

Okay.

Unless I choose it to be. When I first started writing about Great Falls back in about 1983, I'd never been there. But I heard a lot about it because the guy I used to go hunting with used to say how much we needed to go over there and what a neat place it was. But I started putting it in stories because I liked the words "Great Falls," and I liked to put them in a sentence. I would see those words in a sentence and feel the sentence was sort of exotic. But I'd never been there. Over time, I came to know Great Falls and felt a little more sense of responsibility to it, but my sense of responsibility slides along the scales of less to lesser.

For instance, when I was going to set that scene in *Independence Day* at Sally's house, I wanted it to be in Sea Girt, New Jersey. I loved the words "Sea Girt." I didn't know what it meant, but I knew I wanted it in a sentence and so I wrote the scene. And then it was getting close to the time of parting with the book and I thought, hmmm, I better go over there and see Sea Girt. I didn't know why, but some sense of my loving that scene and my wanting its aptness to match the place made me feel responsible. So, I went over there and Sea Girt looked nothing whatsoever like what I had said it looked like. I had misremembered it totally, though I thought I was remembering it well. And the real place wasn't the right place for the scene. So I had to change it to South Mantoloking, which in its own way is an equally unusual name. I liked that pretty well. It isn't as good as "Sea Girt," but the place is more appropriate to the actual place. So I did feel a sense of responsibility. And I wouldn't want to say, for instance, that the Mississippi River flows through Great Falls. I wouldn't want to say that.

As far as attention to cardinal points, I would try to include them by looking at a map. I would rather be right than wrong if it is convenient.

Were you dealing with any of that in "Occidentals" when Charley writes about the streets of Paris without actually having seen them? When he actually gets there, he sees that they're different from what he wrote down, and he has some anxiety about that.

Your romantic fantasies often lead you into a state of being lost. He thought Paris would be one way, but Paris was another. He was acting out on received sensation. I like the idea of characters getting lost. It comes right out of the history of the bildungsroman, people losing their way, losing their baggage, losing their suitcase.

The bildungsroman is a form that seems to come up a lot in your stories. We'll be taken right to the point where the protagonist is supposed to re-

enter with the knowledge he or she has gained—that's where many of your stories leave off, just at the point when we're about to see what happens next.

I just stop where I lose interest. James says human relations never really end. But it's the writer's job to create a geometry which makes them *seem* to end.

Your characters often deal with failed relationships.

I wouldn't say failed. Relationships just don't always come to their expected conclusions. But if you look closely at all relationships, which is what realistic fiction asks you to do about its constituent parts—look closely—you find that there's no such thing as a typical relationship. And because there isn't, there's reason to hope. We suffer when we think of our marriages as a failure, but so often our sense of failure is in response to some norm which never existed to begin with.

Do you see that condition of people moving around from person to person as typical of who we are now?

No. It's just something I made up.

Do you see people having fewer loyalties?

I don't know the answer to that. Fewer loyalties to place, maybe. Fewer loyalties to other people, I hope not. It's hard to do, to have loyalties. Having loyalty may be one of those things one might not be able to do, which is why it's large in the heart of *Independence Day.* First try to define what trust is, which is a function of loyalty. What does trust mean? Does trust mean that my relationship with you obliges you to give up your life for me? Does it oblige you to act against your own best interests for me? Does it mean that you will act in my best interest only if you can? Where is trust along that continuum line?

How has winning the Pulitzer affected your writing, especially in terms of audience?

Well, it has affected it somewhat in terms of my sense of audience. At least in temporary way. I know today is the day when they announce the Pulitzer. I never knew that before I won, though. It's the second Tuesday in April. I didn't know it the day I won it. It made me feel, for a period which I'm sure will end, that there was a curiosity about what I had written and that people would be more inclined to pick up a book of mine. But that was all. If I never go on and write another book—well, I did write another book which sold a lot of copies—but, in time, life will go on and that opening will narrow a little bit, and if I write another really good book, it might open a little more. The Pulitzer itself, I think had a good and wholesome effect on me and on my readership slightly. Well, maybe even more than "slightly enlarged" my readership, but it will size itself back down again eventually. But I was a long time with very few readers, so to have a lot of readers—*Independence Day* sold 400,000 copies, which to me is a lot—that's a whole lot more than I ever expected to sell. I try to be philosophical about those things.

1999

ABOUT THE INTERVIEWERS: **Kevin Kehrwald** received his MA in literature from Arizona State University. At the time of the interview, he was seeking a PhD in American literature at Purdue University. He is a former managing editor at *Sycamore Review*. Interviewer **Lisa Travaglini** was seeking an MFA in fiction at Purdue University at the time of the interview. Her work has been published in *The Dickinson Review*.

RAGE | AMAZON KINDLE | LANDSCAPE AND THE HOME DEPOT| JANE YOUTUBE | HAMILTON WARHOL | IMAGINATION AND RESEARCH | SPACE FOR WRITING

Jane Hamilton

Space for Writing, Imagination and Research, Landscape and the Home Depot, Rage, Warhol and YouTube, Amazon Kindle

Raised in the Chicago suburb of Oak Park, Illinois, and a graduate of Carleton College in Minnesota, Jane Hamilton currently lives in Wisconsin, a state in which all of her published novels have, at least in part, been set. Her short stories have appeared in *Harper's Magazine* and *The Best American Short Stories* anthology. Hamilton's first novel, *The Book of Ruth*, won, among other recognitions, the PEN/Hemingway Award. It became an Oprah's Book Club selection, as did her novel, *A Map of the World*. She has published four other acclaimed novels: *The Short History of a Prince*, *Disobedience*, *When Madeline Was Young*, and, most recently, *Laura Rider Masterpiece*, about a novice writer of romances.

The title character of your newest novel, Laura Rider's Masterpiece, *is an aspiring novelist but a naïve, little-read amateur. How did you inhabit her voice? More specifically, how were you able to portray her ridiculousness without condescending to her sentiments?*

Well I think in the book, actually, no prisoners are taken. The satire's sort of split around equally. You know, after the fact, about last September, I sort of felt that I had, without knowing it—of course how could anyone have anticipated her—I felt that I had channeled Sarah Palin. [*Laughs.*] I mean I was a little worried that … I think … Is it possible to write kind satire? I don't know. I remember reading a review when David Foster Wallace died, some commentary: somebody remarked that he had done all of his satire in a very un-judgmental and kind way, and that just really stuck with me. I'm not sure if that's true and I'm not sure if it's possible because you know, you're exposing ridiculousness and all of the characters in *Laura Ryder* have their absurdities and I just have to say that it was really fun.

Equal opportunity satire.

It was equal opportunity.

Of your now six published novels, four use first-person narration but the latest, along with The Short History of a Prince, *use the third-person. What motivates this style decision? Does a certain voice seem to be present at the outset of your writing, or is that something you work through in revision?*

Well, I think at best it's an intuitive decision. But when I was writing *A Map of the World*, which is in the first-person, two different narrators, I started thinking that I should learn to write from the third-person, and so the first several drafts are in the third-person. The prose is very stiff and it wasn't going well; it wasn't flowing. But I'd read somewhere that you have to earn writing in the first-person because it's easier than the third-person, and in the third-person you have to be the master puppeteer and you have to know everything. You do in the first-person too, but it's more focused. And so I thought "OK, this is an exercise I have to do," but it wasn't right for the book. I sort of feel now that the third-person is maybe a point of view that's for a more "mature" person. It feels more natural to me now and I'm more interested in it. When I was in my twenties, I don't think I was ready for it.

*Along those same lines, in two of your recent novels—*Disobedience and When Madeline Was Young*—the narrators (Henry and Mac, respectively) are primarily observers, arguably not the characters to whom the books' most dramatic action happens. How do you decide from which perspective to tell those stories in particular, or really any of your novels?*

Well, people have said that they wished that *Disobedience* was narrated from the point of view of Elvira, the Civil War re-enacting, gender-conflicted girl. But she really couldn't have told the story because she really wasn't paying attention to what was going on and she's so, you know, she's a bit of a lunatic, and she needs someone to observe her and so it just makes sense to me that the sort of passive observer would be the narrator. But I do have to say that after I finished *Disobedience*, I was so lonesome for Henry Shaw because he amused me. I didn't realize until maybe a couple of years later, when I had to go back and read him for some book club thing, how screwed up he actually was. So you know, I didn't think of him in that light when I was writing it. But I miss him very much, and then I worked for four years on this novel that I had to throw out, which was from the third-person and didn't work at all. And I was still missing Henry and so I think I gravitated towards Mac, the narrator in *When Madeline Was Young* because he's really an older incarnation of Henry Shaw—that passive, observing, wry, slightly depressed ... you know, is there anything better than that kind of a narrator? I don't know...

I realize that it might be sort of a painful subject, but since you just touched on it ... the book that you ended up shelving, which you worked on for some time. When did you realize that it was not working and is it anything you might ever return to?

I don't know about you and your writing life, but I always have a sinking feeling in certain parts of the process—it's terrible, but I had that sinking feeling every single day for four years and every day I felt like throwing up. I mean when it's going well for me, there's kind of a bodily pleasure, an all-is-well-ishness, physically. But I really didn't know what else to do with myself. I really did think about nursing school, you know really trying to do something useful. But do you realize that I would have to take prerequisites? [*Laughs.*] I do not know how to solve for *x*, so I probably would have to go *way* back. So you know that seemed sort of unrealistic. So I just kept working at it and then I was giving a reading at Hope College. This was in Holland, Michigan and I'm going along, very nice reading series in an old movie theater … reading, from this thing. The minutes are ticking by, and I'm thinking "This is the worst thing that has ever been written, and I hate this." And I'm going along calmly but there's heat rising in my face, and I had to read it out loud before but I *really* knew in that moment, and I was just about to hand it in, I'd said to my editor that it's almost done, and so I went back to the hotel really in a panic—"What am I going to do?" —and so I determined that night, that sleepless night, that I would go home and I would write one more draft and I would make it the best failure I could, and I did that. I have a very generous husband who, although I think he would prefer to just read the book to himself, lets me read it out loud to him, which is really important. I mean I read the book out loud to myself, but there's something that happens with his ear in the room where even before I've said the sentence I know what's wrong with it, where I didn't even before think there was anything wrong with it. Anyway so as the nights passed and I was reading this thing, he just sunk lower and lower into his chair. [*Laughs.*] And so I got about halfway through and he just mirrored what I knew and I said, "Thank you; our work is done here." So I put it away and it was the happiest day of my life. It was like finally, you know, really finally leaving the abusive partner. [*Laughs.*] And the only reason I really could leave the bad husband was because I had finally gotten another idea, and so it was as if there was a new man in the wings. I feel that everything leads to the next thing, so the only thing I could do to get to the next thing was to continue writing that failed novel. I mean four years is a long time; it was also after 2001 and it seemed very frivolous to be writing about people who were examining their navels when clearly the paradigm had shifted. So it really was not fun. [*Pauses.*] And will I ever use parts of it? I haven't looked at it really since I've put it away but I think it's unlikely. The sentences are very nice.

So you don't think you'll find yourself ever cherry-picking any ideas or even sentences from that particular project?

No, I think it's doubtful. I used to think that nothing was wasted but now I think that lots of things are wasted. [*Laughs.*]

But it leads to the next thing, so it's all working out.

Exactly.

Back to your characters, and this idea of perspective. You've chosen to write in the voice of characters that often vary wildly from another, and I assume from you, in terms of their age, social class, education, and so on. Do any of these differences, particularly in writing from a male point of view, which you've done in several books, present any specific challenges for you?

Well, I think the danger when you're writing from the opposite gender is that you think you have to represent *all* men or *all* teenagers and of course the challenge with any character is having that character be true to himself. And so, you know, I think my male characters tend to be more in touch with their feminine side than *maybe* the average male, although I can't say. But you know I feel it's been a privilege to write from the male point of view. Henry Shaw, the teenager: I used to think that, as a woman, my gender was right, clearly. But writing from a 17-year-old who is looking at his middle-aged mother, I realized what a trial we are to mankind. And women talk a lot! We're emotional. And so I had a whole new tenderness open up for what it is to be men living among women.

Because your books are usually set in the Midwest, specifically in the Chicago area or in rural Wisconsin, in these areas that are familiar to you, a reader of yours might assume that you "write what you know." But it seems that there is a certain amount of study that goes into these worlds that you create, like the world of a reenacted Civil War battlefield, or the dairy farm or the brain-damaged woman who's visiting the Italian piazza where she had been in her youth, things like that. What is the relationship between your imagination and the type of research you might do for your writing?

Well, I think that although we live in a mall culture and you can go to Santa Barbara and go to Home Depot, and you can go to New York City and go to Home Depot, actually the idioms are very different and the landscape shapes our identity and all of that. So if I were going to set a whole book in say, Michigan, it would be a fairytale because I don't really know the idioms and I think that I would have to live there to really know them. I was at a dinner party with Richard Ford and he was talking about *the* Whole Foods. We say "Whole Foods," no "the." I mean that seems like a kind of significant distinction. So all those little things I wouldn't know about. I feel that there's enough in my Midwestern communities to keep me going for a while. But of course everything is imagined and when I've written about Oak Park where I grew up, I always call it something else because I don't want to have to be true to it. So in a way, that community is a fairytale location also.

Almost all the biographical information about you references your orchard farmhouse, which sounds like the most absolutely idyllic environment for a writer.

We have a lot of mold that just grows and it's ground into putty, so we can't really get rid of it. We have to take the putty out. So yeah, very idyllic. [*Laughs.*]

[Laughs.] Well, that was my question: Is it really idyllic and what's your space for writing like there?

Well, it's evolved: my space for writing has evolved. My husband is the third generation in his farming family and in the fourth generation, that's when it all goes to hell. So stay tuned. [*Laughs.*] So there are several houses; it's kind of like the Kennedy compound and there's this great manor house that was built in 1910, which my husband and I don't live in; we live in the servants' quarters that's across the road, and so it was one of those houses that was built in 1860 and squares were added on as the family needed a little bit more space. So in the beginning when I was married I worked at a little desk in the bedroom because there wasn't much space. I would go away for the weekend and I would come home and my good husband who'd been taking care of everything would have let the children make a tent fort with my desk, which would make me *insane* because that was my little corner, so you know that was bad. And then I got a grant from the Wisconsin Arts Board and I rented a little storefront in a strip mall in a town nearby and I was between the travel agent and the hairdresser's, and then there was me. The travel agent—I don't know what she thought I was doing—but she would often knock on my door, and I was brought up to be sweet and nice, and ask me if I could go to McDonald's to get her lunch. [*Laughs.*] Anyway so that was great because it was just, I had my space, and then later we added on more to the house, so now I have my own little room. In the last ten years, I've had one place for my books and that's really lovely.

But what saved me as a young writer and having young children was going to the Ragdale Foundation in Lake Forest, Illinois. It's a place where writers can go to do their work. It's a big old estate with beautiful, faded gentility and you just get your room and there's a cook who makes dinner and you're with people who are also trying to be quiet so that was *really* important. I would go for maybe two weeks at a time and just put my head down, and then I'd look up two weeks later. And what was great about it was just being able to keep my thread going. I think one of the difficult things, especially about having young children and/or a job is if you can't work every day, you spend a lot of time in the hour or two that you can work trying to remember where you were and what's going on, whereas even if you have just an hour every day you've got that thread going and so you can just write. But I have to say, when I was younger I was enraged—I was enraged nonstop—that I didn't have space. I wanted to have children and that was my choice and I *love* them and *all* of that, but I just really didn't have the time and space to do this thing that I wanted to do, and so I feel like that rage really fueled the work and I would have a half an hour and just do it, and there was very little wasted time in terms of the work and I feel like there was kind of a volcanic pressure that kept it going. And now you know, the children are grown, I have this lovely little space, and the luxury of being able to do work means there's a different quality to it because I am not enraged. And I think sometimes when you reach middle-age, you're not enraged anyway. There's sort of an acceptance that you could say was serenity. So it's just interesting to biochemically have that whole different feeling about the work. The fuel part is different.

So having spent time at some place like Ragdale, do you find it's useful to have a community of people that you've known from places like that? Do you have a writers' community that you consider yourself a part of?

I think I kid myself that one of the important fuels for writing is loneliness, and when I was younger all my stories were about lonely school girls and I wrote for a kind of solace and companionship. I think it's an old fashioned idea that the writer is alone and wrestling in solitude, and I believe in that but I also know that I have a really rich community of writer friends. They don't live where I live but we see each other, we're connected via email. To me, I would say theoretically, a writers' community sounds oxymoronic—writers' community? Writers don't have communities: they're lonely souls. But that's not really the truth, for me.

Are there certain writers, either long-gone writers, up-and-coming writers, or anywhere in between, that you feel a certain kinship with?

Absolutely. I would hope that if there's a heaven and you go through the pearly gates, provided you get there: I would hope that God has the voice of Willa Cather, that sort of very cold look at the world that's infused nonetheless with a deep compassion. So Cather's been really important to me, and I love that feeling of reading a book, whether it's a dead author or a living one, where it's just so good that it restores your faith that novels will continue, and not that necessarily you want to write that book but you want to create that feeling for yourself in your own work. It's just so rich and good and well-crafted and radiantly inspiring.

Do you anticipate your audience when you're writing, particularly given that your newest book is a departure from your other books: although they've had comedic moments, this is your first full-blown light-hearted comedy.

I'm sure everyone's experienced this in writing, whether you're a poet or a fiction writer: you can't help but draw from life and you try to layer it, and give Annabelle black hair rather than blond hair, and stick her in California rather than in Indiana, but there is the fear that Annabelle will see herself and be offended. I've had so many different reactions and I've been afraid that so-and-so will see herself and be upset, and by the same token someone will say, "Well, I saw myself in your book" and is it better to say, "You have not been on my radar for twenty years?" or just nod sweetly? I don't know. I feel like there's no anticipating how or what a person will see in the work. Have you read this essay? Jane Smiley wrote a wonderful essay called "Can Writers Have Friends?" and in it she talks about how although Annabelle might see herself, really what the writer is doing is using the mole on her cheek and her stutter, and plugging it into something that is really for the use of the writer's own idea and it's illuminating the writer's idea, but it's really not about Annabelle. So Jane Smiley goes through this whole argument and then at the end she says, "But I hope that if somebody ever writes about me and uses my details, I will remember what I've said on this matter." So I think it's very dicey business.

I just enjoyed writing this book so much and it gave me so much pleasure. I was really doing it for my own solace. I know that there's people, for example, who really enjoyed *A Map of the World* and for them, that is the book of mine that they like, and I think any book after that has been a disappointment to them. So if they read this, this will just be another in a series that isn't *A Map of the World.* But you can't keep writing the same book. I couldn't possibly write that book again. So you know, we can only do what we do each time.

Laura Rider's Masterpiece *is offering a humorous take on this climate that we're in where even the most unstudied or ungifted amateur can find the Warhol-predicted 15 minutes of fame via reality TV and YouTube and all the media that we have access to. Is this something that, aside from the comedic and satirical tone that you take in your book, you have serious concerns about in terms of the future of literature or culture in general?*

Yes. Especially for your generation. I just wonder how the gift of writers will bubble up through this murk of *all* these voices. And who's really going to—I mean if there are more writers writing novels than there are readers … When I go into the chain bookstores I just think, Who's going to read all these books? I can't stand it. I was recently with a writer friend and we walked into a chain and she said, "Do you enjoy going to bookstores anymore?" and I thought, "No! No, I can't stand it! I feel like I'm going to suffocate." And I'm filled with a panic and I feel like: Who is going to buy these books? It's my responsibility, I love books, I want to support writers, so I have to buy every single new novel on the shelf and I'm counting through my billfold: one, two, three, five dollars, ten. So it's just overwhelming; it's alarming.

Flannery O'Connor said that there are so many people now writing capable stories that the capable writer is sort of killing the form. It's a very cranky sentiment, but I've read for the PEN/Faulkner and the PEN/Hemingway prize and the NEA grants and there's this whole gray middle of really good work, and there's maybe two or three that just blow your circuits. I just hope that with the Web and how far-reaching and dense it is, the voices that we need to hear will bubble up. So yeah, it is a concern and I think there'll always be writers and I think that we will find the gifted writers but I'm not so sure that those people will be able to earn a living. We've been in a great bubble where many of us have been able to actually earn a living, even though I was told again and again, "Don't think that you can do this as a profession; it won't work out; it's really difficult." But through serendipity, and I'm dogged, and I'm at my desk every day and I work, but still I never planned that and that's been a great luxury and privilege and I just hope that there are people for whom that'll still be possible. You know when they talk about Amazon Kindle and they want to make every book $4.99 and get rid of the editors; everybody needs an editor. Everybody needs an editor. And I'm sure you've had the experience of reading any number of books where you think, Where was the editor? You know, a hundred pages can be gone. So, many concerns. But life is always changing and I was reading this history of poetry, and in 1470 or something, the printed book had been around for 30 years and there's this letter that somebody wrote to somebody else saying, "I really fear that the end of the printed word is here." So we've been worried about it forever. I have a son who is a computer person and he tells me that the book will survive. He doesn't want to read on the computer and he doesn't want to read a Kindle and that gives me heart because if *he* says that, then maybe there's hope.

2009

ABOUT THE INTERVIEWER: Originally from Erie, PA, **Erin Blakeslee** earned her MFA in creative writing (fiction) from Purdue University in 2009. During her time at Purdue, she served as an editorial assistant for *Sycamore Review* and, in 2008-2009, as the journal's nonfiction editor. Her short stories and screenplays have been recognized by her university's Literary Awards and the National Society of Arts and Letters, and she has earned several honors for her teaching. She currently teaches composition and creative writing at a Midwestern community college.

TONE AND SPIRIT | OBSESSIONS | READING AND MUSIC AND SPORTS | **NICK**
IS THIS NORMAL? | **HORNBY**
THE DAVINCI CODE | TELLING PEOPLE SECRETS | THE CULTURAL ELITE | HOW BOOKS SURVIVE

Nick Hornby

Tone and Spirit, Obsessions, Reading and Music and Sports, The Cultural Elite, How Books Survive, The DaVinci Code, Telling People Secrets, Is This Normal?

Nick Hornby is the author of the bestselling novels *Slam, A Long Way Down, How to Be Good, High Fidelity*, and *About a Boy*, and the memoir *Fever Pitch*. He is also the author of *Songbook*, a finalist for a National Book Critics Circle Award, *Shakespeare Wrote for Money*, and *The Polysyllabic Spree*, and editor of the short story collection *Speaking with the Angel*. A recipient of the American Academy of Arts and Letters' E. M. Forster Award, and the Orange Word International Writers' London Award 2003, Hornby lives in North London.

There seems to be a mutual obsession between U.S. and British culture. When were you first aware of it, and how does it affect your work?

Which particular obsession? There's music, cinema, books. Growing up, contemporary American writing struck me as fresher, more direct, demotic. There's a spate of American writers I discovered: Anne Tyler, Raymond Carver, Richard Ford, Lorrie Moore. I think it gets filtered through, that influence. I had a brief correspondence with Anne Tyler. She was very complimentary of *High Fidelity.* She said, 'I wouldn't be able to spot the slightest influence.' And I guess to her, it must have looked pretty strange, this novel about an Englishman running a record shop and being obsessed with rock and roll, which didn't have anything to do with anything she's written. But it's about tone and spirit, not about language and subject matter. I knew what was in there.

You write a lot about music and sports. What are some other obsessions? Do you think you write because of your obsessions or do they develop because you write?

The obsessions definitely predate the writing. I'd say those are my big things: reading and music and sports. If you are obsessed with music, then you come to value things outside of work. I was never really very career-oriented. And it was partly because what I did in my spare time meant much more to me than what I was doing in my working time. Until I found a way to incorporate the spare time into the working time. I had a real impetus to do it. There was a lot of desire to try and do something that was more hanging out than working.

What do you think drives you to write about popular culture?

I'd kind of ask the reverse question: why do so many people not write about it? I don't know too many people who have no connection to it. In fact, most people I know have a pretty big connection to it, and it seems to me that actually not enough books reflect that. It seems weird not to have popular culture in books, because that means it doesn't reflect anyone I know.

The terms 'popular' and 'literary' are almost always used exclusively. Why don't they meet, or do they?

I think they do meet when there are literary successes that transcend literary origins, as it were. We can all name books which have sold millions that we deem to have literary merit. I have to say, the older I get, and the more I work in the territory, the more confused I get about what it means: popular versus literary and what defines a literary novel and so on and so forth. A lot of things seem to be defined as literary either because they sell below a certain number, or because they've achieved a certain level of antiquity. Dickens, who was not a literary novelist, I guess, is now a literary novelist. And Jane Austen, who was not a literary novelist, is now a literary novelist. You see what I mean? These definitions didn't exist then. It's a relatively new phenomenon.

I think it probably happened with modernism. For the first time, there was the idea of a readership that would not be a common readership. [Oxford Professor] John Carey wrote a book called *The Intellectuals and the Masses* about modernism where he argued that previously the ability to read and write was in itself the definition of being educated. So you didn't have to worry about the masses because they couldn't read any of this stuff. With mass education, everybody being able to read and write, the cultural elite started to get worried about being encroached upon. There weren't enough ways to define their turf. So they started speaking in this code, which was modernism, basically, and along comes Virginia Woolf. With that, you have the idea of the popular novel and the literary novel possibly for the first time ever. Because none of the people, at least none of the ones who survived the nineteenth century, seemed to be particularly exclusive in that way. And then it's something that's developed with mass literacy, a lot more genre writing as the novels developed, and prizes to define literary merit, and all of these things feed into separating these two apparently different strains of writing.

I've noticed in my own career, for a time, anyway, I was more 'literary' in America than I was in England. I think it was not because Americans have different notions of what literature is, but because my book sales were below a certain level in America and in England they were always above that level. It's very interesting to see what difference it makes to the perception of your work.

You were on the New York Times best-seller list recently.

Right, for *A Long Way Down.* I'm not a literary writer anymore; I'm just a normal writer now. I don't mind either way because these distinctions have stopped making any sense to me at all. I think that the only things probably worth talking about are whether a book has an audience and whether a book survives. And the rest is all hot air. I've stopped believing in any objective principle. I think we all buy into it, that some books are better than other books. But if you start to try and create some overarching principle that would govern all this, it all starts to fall down.

I was trying to write an essay before I came away which was in part about a history of *The Da Vinci Code* and its reception. It seems to have gotten a lot worse as Dan Brown's sales have gotten into the billions. In 2004, I was finding writers in smart broadsheets recommending the book. As a guilty pleasure, but still, you know, 'This is un-put-down-able, blah blah blah,' and then two years later, it's for morons and, what's wrong with the world that all of these people are reading *The Da Vinci Code* and not this other book?

Is that an essay that's going to come out soon?

Yeah, I ended up being rude about some people, so I might have to reconceive it. I write this column ["Stuff I've Been Reading"] for *The Believer,* and my publishers are hoping to bring them out as a collection. This will be the introduction. My big revolution in my personal reading habits is not to read things that bore me anymore, and it's been fantastic. And they're so easy to spot in advance.

What tips it off?

Well, it has to come with the packaging of the literary novel, first of all. And that's my highest risk category. I think it's probably everyone's highest risk category, the literary novel. We know when we pick it up that there is a chance that it will be dull and opaque, and it might wish to draw more attention to its language than the world that it wishes to portray. Those are books that I struggle with, as someone who's got a job and three children and whose reading time is limited. I don't want to get bogged down in a book where I'm reading a paragraph or two paragraphs a night. I don't read very much genre fiction. I read probably more nonfiction than I did. I read more older fiction than I did. And I haven't read anything that I've hated in quite a long time as a result. It's becoming my area of real interest, popular versus literary.

You've been called "the maestro of the male confessional" and a diarist in mix tape form. Do you feel any sort of resulting pressure from labels like that?

The only pressure I feel is not to write another book like that. If I see someone attempting that kind of label, then I feel like I have to be careful. I don't want to repeat myself. I don't want to tread too much in the same territory again. I've only written one book that was a male confessional, which was my first book. And it seems to me that you can only confess things that are true. You can write a fictional confessional, because that's what fiction is: telling people secrets. My first two-and-a-half books were about guys, and I just didn't want to do it anymore because there's only so much that you can say within the same territory, and I thought if I'm going to have a career that lasts, not just commercially but in terms of what's going to keep me stimulated and focused, then I wanted to write about other things. Now I think I just write about people, not one thing or another thing.

In your latest book, you have four first person narrators. Was it difficult inhabiting so many different voices?

It was difficult in the conception of it to ensure at least to my own satisfaction that the voices seemed distinct. I didn't want the reader to keep flipping back to the beginning of the chapter to see who was talking. But on the other hand, you don't want it so contrived that they speak in wildly different ways when in fact people don't speak in wildly different ways, by and large. I edited a book called *Speaking With the Angel* a few years ago, where I'd asked people to write first person with the possibility that some of them might possibly be performed on stage. I really enjoyed my story. It seemed to come easier than a lot of things happen, and it was partly because I was deliberately using someone's speaking voice rather than any kind of literary voice. And that was something that hung over with this book. I wanted to carry on with that. So the conceit is four monologues rather than a conventional novel in that form.

Do you write many stories?

No. I'd like to write more than I do. But I've got things stacked up. I never anticipated doing so much traveling. I never thought that the books would be so widely translated, and that's a weird thing. When I started, I felt that it was so personal and so focused on a certain area of London, I didn't necessarily think about being published in any other country. You start to rationalize after the fact. Oh, OK, it wasn't as personal and focused on a certain area as I thought it was. After *High Fidelity,* which was my first semi-successful book here in the U.S., I got the impression that after readings and things that people didn't even notice necessarily that it was British. They thought it was about them or about their brothers or their boyfriends or whatever. No one ever said to me, 'Oh, that's what it's like to live in London.'

Russell Banks once said, "Poetry tells us what it means to be human. We're the only species that needs to learn over and over what it means to be itself." I wondered if you had any thoughts on how contemporary fiction teaches us certain things.

Well, isn't it more that we're confused that we're selves? You know, it's a very troubling and problematic thing, to not know where the self begins and humanity ends. The points of which we're representative and the points of which we're peculiar. We fret about this an awful lot, about what's normal. 'Is this normal?' is a running question through therapy, fiction, problem pages in newspapers. It's pretty central. It's a good title for a novel, actually: 'Is This Normal?'

2006

ABOUT THE INTERVIEWER: **Sarah Layden** won the Allen and Nirelle Galson Prize for fiction from *Stone Canoe* arts journal for the short story "Hysterectomy," which was awarded the Kneale Award for fiction at the 2006 Purdue Literary Awards. Her short fiction and poetry can be found in *Artful Dodge, PANK, Margie, Blood Orange Review, The Evansville Review,* and elsewhere. Excerpts from her novel, *Sleeping Woman*, were published by *Freight Stories, Cantaraville*, and the *Dia de los Muertos* anthology. At the time of the interview, she was *Sycamore Review*'s nonfiction editor. Find her online at www.sarahlayden.com.

THE CULTURAL REVOLUTION | CONVENTIONAL CHINESE FICTION | GOOD WORK HABITS | LANGUAGE FOR THE IMMIGRANT | LEISURE AND HARD LABOR AND CREATIVITY

HA JIN

Ha Jin

The Cultural Revolution, Conventional Chinese Fiction, Language for the Immigrant, Good Work Habits, Leisure and Hard Labor and Creativity

Ha Jin left his native China in 1985 to attend Brandeis University. He is the author of the internationally bestselling novel *Waiting*, which won the PEN/Faulkner Award and the National Book Award, and *War Trash*, which won the PEN/ Faulkner Award for Fiction, and was a Finalist for the Pulitzer Prize and the Kiriyama Pacific Rim Book Prize; the story collections *The Bridegroom*, which won the Asian American Literary Award, *Under the Red Flag*, which won the Flannery O'Connor Award for Short Fiction, and *Ocean of Words*, which won the PEN/Hemingway Award; the novels *The Crazed* and *In the Pond*; and three books of poetry. His latest novel, *A Free Life* is his first novel set in the United States. He lives in the Boston area and is a professor of English at Boston University.

One of the great horrors of the Cultural Revolution was the persecution and murder of teachers by their students. You bemoan this tragedy in poems like "In a Moonlit Night," and "A Thirteen-Year-Old Accuses His Teacher." Yet "The Fight," depicting the play sword fight between a father and his son, closes with the lines: "To grow is to learn how to fight back. */ I am your teacher, your rival, / the one doomed to be wrecked." Do you think, on some basic level, an artist must overthrow his or her master to know a truer self?*

Not necessarily. You don't have to kill the father to become a father yourself. No, I think influence is always a good thing. I think great writers often have an energy and a strength that's there, and for me it is always a privilege to borrow something from them. That doesn't mean you just follow them. You can go further than them. But you don't have to kill them, you don't have to smack them down. It's impossible, in fact. There are writers like Hemingway, who said he'd already defeated Turgenev and could go a few rounds with Tolstoy. But you can't kill them. They stay. They are great writers. They are giants and they are there. Just learn from them, and try to do something different.

Everyone talks about the Western influences in your writing. They mention the Russians, of course, and Hemingway. But I'd like to look at the Chinese influences. I know you quoted from Lu Xun in your first book, Between Silences*—that seems obvious. Out of the Chinese tradition, what other writers have influenced you or continue to move you?*

In fiction, not many. Only Lu Xun. Because fiction written in Chinese, in modern times, is a Western form, not a conventional Chinese form. Conventional Chinese fiction is very different. It is a performance-type art. It is very different from the novel. In poetry, I would say there is more influence. Du Fu, Li Bai, Han Yu, and Xin Qiji are all great poets. In fact, I can't help but be influenced by Chinese poetry. From my early years, I have tried to read as much as I can of these poets—even memorize some of their poems. In Chinese we really do have a very grand poetic tradition. It's very rich.

In a recent interview you argued that "the narrator shouldn't be intrusive" and that "you have to respect the intelligence of the reader." I find that this is more in the rhetorical tradition of Chinese and Japanese writing—at least in expository prose. In the Western tradition the author has to control the reader and argue a point. The Eastern tradition is more open ended and reader-based. So, could your desire not to intrude or control the reader also reflect an Asian influence?

Maybe. In poetry I think we work to make the language suggestive instead of explicit. In fact, even in English literature—in the short fiction—there is a rule: everything should be suggestive, not directly stated. That's a way to respect the reader's intelligence and imaginative power. No writer can write well without that kind of expectation from the reader.

In your interviews, you frequently discuss the question of language for the immigrant. You have stated that the immigrant's life is "always affected by the insufficiency" of not knowing the new tongue and that "Language divides the saltwater and freshwater fish." Perhaps most eloquently, you once stated that "You have to change yourself when you change languages." How has writing in English changed you?

In very subtle ways. When I started, I didn't expect to change. I thought I was just a user of the language, that language was a tool. But in the process I realized there were a lot of things that I didn't care about before that gradually became very valuable to me. Ideas like solitude. Individualism. Self-independence. These things are quite alien in Chinese. Somehow, psychologically, I absorbed these ideas from the English language and they became part of my existence. In that sense, language changes you and makes you different. Also, I feel a deep alienation from Chinese, from Chineseness, from the culture, the history, and the past. That doesn't mean that I don't care about China. I do. But in a different way, not the same as at the beginning, when I was obsessed with China, with writing about China. Now I don't care much about that.

You write in English principally for a North American audience, yet all of your published work to date concerns China. In what ways has your awareness of your North American audience shaped or governed your fiction? Do you present a "stylized" version of China?

I really don't have a sense of audience, honestly. Very often I imagine an ideal audience. I think that's important—having one or two persons in mind as an audience who know English very well and who are well educated in English literature. I think that's enough. The person doesn't have to be American. It can be anybody who knows English and the literature. Sometimes there can be a great writer in your audience. I think in the old tradition, the English poetic tradition, the audience doesn't just exist horizontally, among your contemporaries. There is a sense of a vertical audience, an audience in the past and the future. T. S. Eliot talked about this. When John Berryman was asked "For whom do you write?" he said, "For the dead you love." Very clearly, the audience doesn't have to be a group of contemporaries. It can be imagined. You can study it in that sense.

Some critics in the People's Republic, like Beijing University professor Liu Yiqing, have accused you of treason, of pandering to American stereotypes of China as a primitive, dirty, and violent place. Does this criticism surprise you?

Yes. I had dinner with Liu Yiqing, and I didn't expect it would come from her. Also, if you read her article carefully it is obvious that she didn't read *Waiting* because her review is based on a lot of assumptions. When I started to write in English, I expected responses of this kind. For instance, when Conrad became known in English, some Poles condemned him. I remember one Polish writer said of the British, "They're so rich they have bird's milk. They don't need a writer like you. Why don't you write in Polish?" So I expected this, but when it actually happened it still hurt, like a door slammed on your face.

I find Liu's criticism absurd; it was an ad hominem attack of the lowest sort. I'm curious about how some Chinese critics are obsessed with the historical accuracy of your work. Liu commented on the impossibility of a young female character, such as Shuyu in Waiting, *having bound feet in the 1960s. She claims you are exaggerating "primitive" Chinese traditions.*

But Shuyu is based on a true person. The person is still living in the town where my parents-in-law live now. In fact, three months ago we called my parents-in-law, and the daughter and the first wife still live in the town. I would never give out their names, because then people would go and look at them, but it is factual. There are people who argue that it is impossible, but China is a huge country. In the city, true, very few women have bound feet. But in the countryside, there are all kinds of people.

There is a book by an American journalist, Peter Hessler, entitled *River Town: Two Years on the Yangtze.* Hessler was teaching in China in 1997-98. In the book he mentioned that, in his class, he asked the students how many of their grandparents have bound feet. Most of their grandparents did. That means these grandparents are in their sixties or seventies now. So it's normal. In the countryside, it's normal. That's why Liu's accusation is crazy. Also, the cover of *Waiting*, it's just crazy. Liu observed the cover's image [a long braid of black hair] as a Chinese man's queue, something out of the Qing dynasty. But really it's just the kind of braid commonly worn by women today in China. But even if we take it as a man's queue, the book does have feudalistic residue and customs. So it is not irrelevant, in that respect.

Some readers have hinted at the allegorical quality of Waiting. *The novel flirts with the conventions of the romance novel, and perhaps even the postmodern novel. What drew you to challenge the boundaries of the realism that has, for the most part, governed your work to date?*

I didn't think about the book's genre, or what kind of boundaries the book crossed. What I worried about at the time was how to make the story work, how to make it richer. To be aware of all the possibilities, the subtleties. I was not aware of the novel's allegorical dimensions at the beginning. But in the process of revising it I gradually realized it was a dimension of the story. So it was a process, not something I planned. Even the form—I wrote it as a novella originally, and gradually I realized the material itself had some kind of form. That's why the book has three parts, and each part has twelve chapters. That was the lesson: I realized the material itself had its own form. It's not something I imposed.

"Alive" and "After Cowboy Chicken Came to Town," both from The Bridegroom, *push at the boundaries of the short story genre. Both are lengthy stories with multiple episodes and complex plots—easily material for a novel. In your mind, what constitutes material for a novel, as opposed to a short story? In what ways do the genres differ?*

The form is part of it. Also, whether the material itself has enough centripetal force to unify all the details. I agree, "After Cowboy Chicken Came to Town" could be a small novel. I may have to write it, because some people in California want to turn it into a movie script. I couldn't be involved in it, I was busy then, but their version is so different from my intentions that I may have to write it as a book. If they can make it into a movie, that's fine. If they can't, it's all right with me. But it is subject matter for a novel, that's true.

The distinction between novel and story is not very clear, sometimes. For instance, I started *In the Pond* as a short story. It became too big. It was impossible to put it into a collection, so it became a small novel. Very often, we can tell by the weight of the subject or the material just how many pages it can sustain—if it can sustain the momentum. There are stories, Chekhovian in a sense, that don't really have plots. Just a piece of life. One can measure, in that sense, the form. They don't have the unfolding of the drama, just the richness of that life.

You've spoken about the progression in your fiction, from Ocean of Words *up to* The Bridegroom, *as a kind of movement from the rural toward a more urban sensibility.* Waiting *seems like a kind of turning point in this respect, given that it is equally divided between the rural and the urban. How conscious or deliberate has this larger narrative movement been?*

It has not been a conscious effort. In *Waiting*, I wanted to set some scenes in the countryside, but I didn't have the awareness on that grand scale about my own development as a writer. I just go book by book. But there will be a moment when I get out of China and write a book about that effort of moving toward the West. Honestly, that will be a big jump. I haven't really gotten there myself. I will try to make it, but it will be hard. For me, it is a matter of life or death as a writer because I don't care about China as I used to. I can't write book after book just about China. I may write some books set outside of China, and then gradually in the States. So, that will be a very conscious effort.

In your first book of poetry, Between Silences, *the language and form resemble that of a fine prose sketch—and considering all the dialogue, perhaps even that of a short story with line breaks to mark the spoken rhythms.*

Are you consciously resisting what some have called the "artificial poetic" of over-crafted verse? Were these poems partly the result of a greater commitment to fiction writing that came to dominate your career in the 1990s?

Yes. That's why I wrote *Ocean of Words*. I realized the Army material would be more effective for fiction. In fact, in *Between Silences*, if I remember correctly, in the last section there are some poems that are more lyrical, and not just monologues. I realized some of the monologues were, in fact, better material for fiction. That's why I began to write fiction. The second book, *Facing Shadows*, is different. I think I cherish the lyrical poem, rather than just narrative. But the first book—I wasn't serious. I didn't even know whether I would continue to write in English. There was no intention or deep thinking about the project. I reached a point where I had to write something, so I wrote the poems.

You speak often of poetry as being "pure luck," something you "just try and try" until it works, as if you are subject to the muse. Is that different from the way you conceive of stories? Are you more of a designer or an architect when it comes to fiction?

In fiction, as long as you know you have a good story, you can make it work. If one way doesn't work, you try another way. As long as you are patient and stay with it, you can make it work. With poetry, sometimes it doesn't work. If it started as a strong poem, you can build it as a strong poem. But sometimes it just doesn't work.

Why is that? What is it about the lyric?

It's excessive energy, I guess, an overflow, right? You know, Wordsworth. Sometimes a poem doesn't have that strength, or that emotional intensity. And it is also related to the language and your own meaning. In that sense, poetry depends on luck.

It sounds like you usually have a fairly well-developed sense of a story before you write it. Is writing fiction a question of finding the words to match a preconceived idea or image, or do you, through the process of composition, discover the story's true subject as you write?

For me, I have three or four scenes in my mind. The writing process is to find a way to connect one scene to another. And then also to make the scenes more elaborate. Most of the time I know how it will end. For me, that's very important. From the beginning, you have to know that sense of direction. Most times, I don't write to look for the story. That doesn't mean I just write it. Sometimes a story has to be revised again and again. It's not just the storyline. Other things, other complexities, are not in view yet. So the writing process is a way of fulfilling that material.

Two stories in The Bridegroom *employ collective, or communal, narration: "A Tiger-Fighter is Hard to Find" and "The Woman from New York." What draws you to this particular narrative stance?*

At this moment, the first-person singular is cherished in a writer. But the first person plural is a very different voice. Very often, it has a moral judgment in the voice, like Faulkner's "A Rose for Emily." I learned a lot from that story. The narrator assumes a moral judgment. Also, there is a kind of propaganda in the voice. It highlights the group's similarities and it suppresses differences. It is a "we" voice, very powerful, and also very risky. It can give a lot of subtlety and intelligence to the narration. That's why I'm attracted to that voice.

We really see that in "The Woman from New York." The community totally rejects the woman.

Yes, they are full of prejudice. But sometimes the prejudice can make the voice authentic.

That's certainly the case with Cheng, the protagonist in "The Bridegroom." He is both prejudiced and sympathetic towards Baowen, the homosexual character in the story. Of course, Cheng is also blind to his own homoerotic desires.

And the consequences of his own sympathy, or his own humanity. I deliberately created him as a convincing but prejudiced narrator.

Homosexuality is really not talked about openly in the PRC. Has this been something you've been thinking about? Was there something that moved you to that story?

That story came last. After I finished all the other stories, I realized I needed another story for the collection to enrich it, to make the scope of the collection broader. I thought homosexuality could be a good topic. I read articles and one or two books in Chinese about this topic, and some newspaper pieces. I'm not gay, so I don't know that intimate life—what it's like. So the best way is to have a narrator related to the victim, idiosyncratic and biased at the same time. For me, that is a suitable narrator. So the story was purely willed into existence.

You've written in the voice of a woman, right?

Not very often. Originally, "A Tiger-Fighter is Hard to Find" had a female narrator. It didn't work. The editor at *Oxford American* said, "Why don't we keep this neutral?" It was a good suggestion. We don't know the gender now.

"After Cowboy Chicken Came to Town" is a story about a clash of values: American capitalism versus Chinese communism. In your opinion, what are the pre-eminent misconceptions Americans have concerning China? What are the pre-eminent misconceptions Chinese have concerning America?

Quite often, in this country, we tend to think of the Chinese as one kind. But there are so many kinds. Even in the government, which is considered rigid and hostile. But there are different kinds of people in the government. There are a lot of quite liberal people, and there are many who are very, very conservative. So I think we should keep that in mind, how complex things are. The same is true for the United States. A lot of Chinese people think Americans are decadent, or that American women are very loose. [laughter] It's not true. There are Americans and Americans. Both sides tend to ignore the complexity of humanity.

You once described your second collection of stories, Under the Red Flag, *as a "moral history about that place at that time." Do you feel that your fiction performs some kind of a larger cultural or moral work in that regard?*

At the time I was working on that book a lot of things weren't clear. I did want to write a kind of local history, or a moral history, but I think I took myself too seriously. So the book was intended for that kind of grand scale of things. But it's not. As a moral history, it may not work at all because very few Chinese speak any English. But I do think most of those stories are very authentic. They are decent stories. And, together, they do have that kind of function, to give a history of a place and a group of people.

Along these lines of a writer taking himself too seriously, do you think of yourself as shi*, a member of the literati in the traditional Chinese sense? Do you see yourself as a* special *kind of person?*

No, no. A writer is a worker. A worker with words. That's all. I don't have a sense of superiority. I do think that is a bad mentality among Chinese intellectuals, their sense of the author as a different kind of person, a superior human being. No, I don't have that. I don't think that is necessary. But I do feel it is important to have more privacy, or some isolation, so you can work. More peace and quiet.

As a writer who is also a teacher of writing, how do you feel about the connection between the two practices? Are they mutually beneficial, or does one drain your energy for the other?

Teaching is a kind of burden, honestly. It cuts into your own work, especially when you write fiction. Fiction depends on how much time and energy you put into the manuscript. Teaching uses the same energy. But for a poet, teaching is a great profession. You don't need to sit down for ten hours a day to work on a manuscript of poetry. In fact, you need about one or two hours a day, just your best time. Then you can rest your brain and do something else. For a poet, teaching is really a great, great profession. I can see that. For fiction, it's very different. Especially when you are writing a novel. You have to think about it constantly, you have to live with the characters mentally. So that is hard. That's why I am leaving teaching for some years, so I can write fiction. I will stay in the South and live frugally and write full-time for a few years.

I admire that. There are very few writers who remain free of the academy. Cormac McCarthy comes to mind. In interviews he has talked about the relative simplicity of his life.

For many years, each of his books sold, like, two thousand copies. He just lived in a motel, writing full-time.

As an artist, you are willing to make some sacrifices.

Yes. I think a major lesson for a beginning writer to learn is how to live cheaply. It's very important because you have to conserve your energy and time for the work. That's the most important lesson. There's a lot of cunning in that. How to survive and work. You can get a job with a very big salary, but the money part is not what you really want.

Does it trouble you to say no to an academic career?

Yes, sure. But with a job you have a lot of obligations, things you have to do—meetings and social engagements. That's the disadvantage of winning an award. Suddenly, you have so many requests. It's hard for me to deal with it.

You must get a lot of correspondence and e-mail.

Yes. I really can't handle it. When people know where you teach, anybody can get access to your e-mail. Sometimes they send comments, or they ask you questions. Whatever. There are just too many to deal with. In this sense, Cormac McCarthy is a big influence. I often talk about how influence is not just from the work. Whether or not you like McCarthy's work, if you know the way he lives—that's an influence. That can be an inspiration.

There's a lot of discussion these days about electronic publishing, e-texts, on-line books, and the like. Do you have any ideas about the future of publishing and the World Wide Web?

I think the book will remain. The number of books published may be lower, but the book will survive. I'm not worried because I don't write to make money. The labor you put into a book is not comparable with the money you can make from it. In that sense, it's not that important to me.

In the Pond *is a comedy.* Waiting *is a tragedy. What challenges does each mode present to a writer?*

Really, you don't think, "This is a comedy. How do I make this funny?" or, "This is a tragedy. How do I make this sad?" That material came with different emotional qualities. You respond to it differently. You deal with it differently. *In the Pond* came as a kind of sickness. I read a two-page article about a policeman who was also an amateur painter. He was oppressed by his superiors for many years, and eventually he prevailed through his painting. I was made sick by that article. It was depressing to me, at the time. Should art be used like this? I wrote the novel to cope with my personal feeling of nausea, and to try to be comic. But *Waiting* is different. It is a tragic story. I was more serious. In other words, I was more sympathetic to most of the characters in the book. Whereas the author of *In the Pond* is much more detached.

In the Pond *is, on the one hand, a Künstlerroman affirming the power of individual artistic expression. It is certainly one of your most eloquent examples of politicizing the personal. On the other hand, one might argue that Bin never truly understands the depth of his potential; he is, perhaps, too quick to settle for too little. Is this a reflection of his character, or are you commenting on the power of art to change a person?*

Both. He's that kind of person. Very practical and very talented, but he doesn't know where to go. Also, this book is about spiritual imprisonment. Everything is perceived in utilitarian terms. Art as a means of personal or political gain. That's very conventional in Chinese literature and language. Artists are supposed to be useful. But Bin is half-educated. He's self-educated. There are a lot of intellectuals like that. Satisfied with very little. In that sense, it's also a kind of social comment.

You published two volumes of short stories before publishing your first novel. Has writing novels influenced your sense of the story's form or aesthetic?

I understand the story better. I realize it's much harder to write a short story. The labor involved in a volume of short stories is sometimes much more than in a novel. That's why, as long as I can, I always avoid writing a short story. It's very scary. [laughter] You finish one piece, and then a book needs another ten stories. It's really very demanding, and very hard. But if you just write short stories while you are teaching, then you can do both simultaneously. But for a novel, it's very hard.

What do you have to do to prepare yourself to write a novel? Do you need to block out time or secure a place for yourself?

You don't prepare. You just do it, just follow the process. You know the ending, or the last line. And you just do it. Mostly it's just getting black on white. Then you have something to work on. For me, I have some other manuscripts. Every one of them was started under pressure—you know, if you don't do this, you'll get in trouble. So you do something, and it becomes very big, and you realize, "This is a novel." And you can't finish it, so you put it aside.

You have a very workmanlike attitude toward writing. I've heard you say that the writer is merely an instrument or a tool that produces the work.

I think good material has its own form or demands. Very often, the writer does not feel equipped with the ability to meet those demands. That's why we try to develop good work habits, in order to realize all the possibilities of that material. In that sense, we serve a mission. When a writer works, he wants to make the work better than himself. That's why I think we should make the separation between the writer and the work. The writer is not that important. It's the work. If the work is good, we'll give some credit to the writer. But we shouldn't reverse this. Sometimes, we treat the writer more seriously than the work.

Do you ever reflect on your past work and think, "That's great?"

No. Never. I'm just tired of it. Honestly. I don't really return to my work. When I have to read it, I will read it. Otherwise, I don't return to it. I'm just really tired of it. I think, to date, I can say that for every book I've done my best. That's all. I can comfort myself with that. But, eventually, whether I can continue to do that—that's a question mark. Because the demands are much greater. I have much less time. I don't have the leisure. Before the National Book Award, I could spend a few years with each book. But now things are speeding up. It's hard. It's very hard to do.

What I hear you talking about throughout our conversation today is the issue of the artist in the marketplace. Winning the National Book Award, for example, has placed a certain amount of pressure on you. What are your thoughts on the writer's relationship to the market? Is it something to treat warily, or is it something a writer can utilize or manipulate for his own advantage?

You can't think of how to sell a book. You can't think of what is popular, or what people are reading. Believe me, not all publishers want you to do that. I made a terrible mistake when I met my editor for the first time. This was the first time my book had been accepted by a trade publisher. My editor took me to lunch and I asked her what she expected me to write. She was shocked. She said, "You just pick out whatever you want to write. I can't give you a subject." I excused myself, and said, "Yes, the subject will come from within. It won't be imposed from outside." But I didn't expect that. Later, I had lunch with another editor at Pantheon who said, "Our job is just to find the best fiction and to publish it." So, there are still some presses who don't just publish popular stuff. True, they publish some. But on the other hand they are interested in serious literature.

When you're composing, are you able to be your own best editor? Or is it still important to show your work to other people?

I think it's good, if you have good friends. I don't have that kind of person. I live in a kind of isolation in Georgia. The only people I show my manuscript to, when I feel it is presentable, are my agent and my editor. Usually, they respond with one page, with suggestions and questions and ideas. Things like, "Maybe this character is not sharp enough." Then I revise the manuscript in response to their comments. Most of the time, after that, the manuscript is ready. But that means before I presented it to them I had revised it a dozen, two dozen, three dozen times.

When Toni Morrison spoke at Purdue last year, she tried to dispel the myth that artists must endure chaotic, painful, or dangerously edgy lives in order to be creative and productive. Yet you talk very explicitly about work produced under intense pressure—for you it was a matter of a job, an income to support your family. You also allude to Du Fu and Li Bai as "two great poets who had the bitterest lives," and voice your own fears about the soft dangers of an America life where "Once I have the freedom to say / my tongue will lose its power / How can I speak about coffee and flowers?" How significant is environment to a writing life? Can comfort and success silence an artist?

When I wrote that poem, I was thinking different things. I still had a Chinese mindset. But there is a lot to be said about America. Leisure is, I believe, vital to creativity. How many talents were lost or destroyed by hard labor? I don't think American life will suppress one's creativity. Also, I think it is a good advantage to have access to great literature. Those things are more important than just having a sense of frustration or being victimized.

Do you think it is a myth that great writing comes out of great suffering?

I think it is a misperception. How many Chinese have suffered? How many great books were written? We don't lack victims. What we lack, really, are the artists and the books.

2002

ABOUT THE INTERVIEWERS: **Rob Davidson** is an Associate Professor of English at California State University, Chico. He is the author of *Field Observations*, a collection of short stories, and *The Master and the Dean: The Literary Criticism of Henry James and William Dean Howells*. He received an MFA in creative writing and a PhD in American literature from Purdue University, where he was the editor-in-chief of *Sycamore Review*. Interviewer **Henry Hughes** is the author of two collections of poetry, *Men Holding Eggs* (2004 Oregon Book Award) and *Moist Meridian*. He teaches at Western Oregon University and regularly contributes to *Poetry Northwest* and *Harvard Review*. In 1988, he served as *Sycamore Review*'s first editor.

PRESSURE | WORKING
AND WRITING | CHILDREN
UNDERGROUND | NAMI
EMPATHY | AVON | MUN
PLAYWRITING | GAPS

Nami Mun

Working and Writing, Pressure, Gaps, Children Underground, Playwriting, Avon, Empathy

Nami Mun was born in Seoul, South Korea, and grew up there and in Bronx, New York. She has worked as an Avon Lady, a street vendor, a photojournalist, a waitress, an activities coordinator for a nursing home, and a criminal defense investigator. After earning a GED, she earned a BA in English from UC Berkeley and an MFA from University of Michigan, where she won a Hopwood Award for fiction. She has received a Pushcart Prize, and scholarships from Yaddo, MacDowell, Eastern Frontier, Squaw Valley, *Tin House* Writers Conference, and the Key West Literary Seminar. Her stories have been published in the *2007 Pushcart Prize Anthology, Iowa Review, Witness*, and other journals, including *Tin House*, which named her an Emerging Voice of 2005. *Miles from Nowhere*, her debut novel, was short-listed for the Orange Award and selected for Booklist's Editors' Choice. She was named Best New Novelist of 2009 by Chicago magazine and is a recipient of a Whiting Award. She lives in Chicago and teaches creative writing at Columbia College.

One of the fascinating aspects of your writing life is the path you took to the Michigan MFA. By the time you arrived at Michigan, you'd already worked dozens of jobs and published stories in several venues. What were some of the most important lessons you took from these early years of working and writing, and how did this affect your experience at Michigan?

I'd like to think all of my jobs, even the waitressing jobs, were helpful toward thinking about character and voice. My job as criminal defense investigator was by far the juiciest; juicy details came out of that. I got to meet and speak with, on a daily basis, a variety of people from different strata of society. Basically, they would all be talking about this one crime—whatever the case was I had—and I would interview the defendant, a defendant's family member, a witness, a cop, and an attorney. We're always talking about that one crime, but I'm getting different people's perspectives on that incident. So I got to hear the same content, but from different voices. I got to really hone in on how people speak—the syntax and word choice they used, their gestures and point of view. All of that really helped with my writing.

When I got to Michigan, the first thought was, "Oh, thank God I don't have to work anymore." That was really just a great relief. Being in an MFA program allowed me to just think about literature and writing and my book, whereas before, I was doing whatever jobs that came up just to make money so I could keep writing. I've had a couple of jobs where I would work really intensely for six months, and then quit, and then write for a few months, working off my savings and such. What the MFA program gave me was sort of a stable, rigorous, structured lifestyle, which was kind of nice. And even teaching actually helped with writing because teaching undergrads and introductory classes, I had to go back to the basics of writing. And that allowed me to think about my own work just sort of very simply and cleanly.

But that said, I think it was really good that I went into an MFA program having a body of work already underway because I didn't feel the pressure that I think some of my colleagues felt, writing fresh stories and turning them in. I had stories already that I was sort of happy with, and I could turn those in for workshop, and get the sort of final workshop edits. I call them 80 percent stories. I felt like they were 80 percent done and needed that 20 percent of comments from other people to really tighten the work, and while I was doing that I was writing new stories so I didn't feel pressure to rush those stories. I'm a very, very slow writer. And so knowing that about myself—knowing that I don't write well under pressure—I was happy that I already had a body of work that I could turn in for workshops.

Obviously, as the title Miles from Nowhere *suggests, your protagonist Joon is very much alone in the world. Her interactions with others are often fleeting, and at times violent. In a novel with such an isolated protagonist, how did you forge so many moments of connection—I'm thinking here, for example, of the conclusion of "Shelter," where the characters seem both incredibly isolated, but also linked—even if that connection is more disturbing than tender?*

You're talking about a scene where they run up to the burned-out building and they've stolen this Christmas tree, and the three characters are sort of sitting around.

I often feel that you might be with someone, or a lot of people, and you do have these tiny moments of connection, but then you can have this double consciousness where you realize that deep down you're actually alone at the same time, a sort of dichotomy where you exist on both planes. I think the title *Miles from Nowhere* parallels this in the sense that Joon is in New York City in the 1980s. There are millions of people. It's a city of everything—you have access to culture, nightlife, film, art, music, and all of these people with different languages, such an array of things that you have access to, but here's Joon who is in the middle of all this, and she feels absolutely alienated and isolated. To her, NYC could be Hammond, Indiana. She doesn't have access to these things. She actually doesn't have the capability of going to see a concert, or even visiting family.

I wanted to play around with that feeling of having everything around you, but being absolutely alone within it. I think Joon feels that with people, with human beings. She can have a lovely moment with two other characters and a tree that looks like it has just been picked up from the garbage dump, and feel close, like she has this family for a moment, but then at the same time realize that she is very much alone.

Joon's relationship, or lack of a relationship, with her mother and father is at the margins of the story throughout. In large part her parents are the reason she left home. They are rarely on the page, yet their presence seems to permeate the entire story in very haunting ways. How did you accomplish that?

I'm a strong believer in gaps; gaps in between sentences and stories and chapters. Joy Williams is another writer who I feel has these wonderful gaps between some of her sentences, and some of her stories. Where the leap is not such a huge leap that you can't make a connection with the next sentence, but it is sort of an off-kilter leap where you're left to wonder about that space a little bit more, and you have to sort of fill in as the reader what that gap doesn't mention. Some authors like to come in at 80 percent and have readers meet them at 20 percent. I think of myself as a 50 percent person. My ideal reader has to come in and meet me halfway. They have to do a lot more of the work to read what's not on the page, to think about and feel what's not on the page.

Joon is a teen narrator, and teen narrators are often considered unreliable in the sense that they can't express their emotions. She is definitely a stunted narrator in that she's not going to go around telling you how she feels. So my reader has to fill in those gaps, and that's I think what you're talking about as a reader. You're filling in the gaps between the family scenes.

I was very careful about where I placed the family scenes, actually. When I was done with the book, I drafted this spreadsheet. I listed every story, what years the story took place, what the flashback scenes were, all the pop cultural references, what the seasons were, the newspaper references, what's making the present action. I wanted to make sure that the family stories came in at a certain interval, so that you didn't completely forget about them. I wanted to create this rhythm about the family; she's always thinking about them. Hopefully readers are able to fill in the space between using their own imaginations, and my writing—the actual sentences—are just sort of guiding them to what they should think about next.

Many of the chapters in the book were published in short story form prior to Miles from Nowhere. *You've described each story as being like a cog in a larger narrative arc, and you've said that, at a point, you had to "undo" some of the short stories. Can you speak about that process?*

I was treating the stories as self-contained pieces, and often I would send them out for publications and such, so in each story I had to introduce Joon again so that a reader who hasn't read any of the other stories could understand what was happening, that she was a runaway. So, some of that definitely had to be taken out. But each story had to have its own purpose for the larger narrative, so I would have to put in certain things to create that narrative arc. Here's a good example: For "Club Orchid," which is the first story that I wrote, the original version didn't have any of the family elements except for a few lines here and there, but I had to completely throw in this family element because by that point in the book we needed to know that she was still thinking about her parents. So, all of the family and father scenes and such had to be put in. Certain things about the setting and the time period I had to take out, because they weren't necessary anymore, because at this point you're a third of the way into the book, you know you're in the '80s, you can tell by a few of the song choices I put in the club scene: Michael Jackson, those kind of details. I had to be careful about not over-mentioning certain parts of the narrative arc, and not under-mentioning others.

Joon's date in "Club Orchid" is a perfect example of how your novel is populated with characters that are not exactly likable. Yet they never feel villainized by the author, or portrayed in any unsympathetic way. When you're creating these scenes, how do you go about entering these characters and making them sympathetic? Does that just have to do with Joon's perception, or is it your own? Is this an exercise in point of view, or does it reflect your own observations of the world?

Joon has such an immense capability to feel a lot of sympathy for people around her. I like her because of that. I guess empathy is more like it; it's not like she sits around and coddles characters, but I think she sort of tries to see what lies inside each character.

When I was a criminal investigator, many of my clients were not people who society would like. These are people who have committed homicide or sexual assault; they're not the prettiest people. For instance, I had this one case where this guy had ended up killing someone in a spontaneous fight, and I had to talk to him for hours to not only find out his side of the story, but his entire life story. And you realize that this person is being judged on this one act. He had some misdemeanors and such for public drinking and stuff like that, but he was being judged by this one act, something that he did unto someone else that was violent, yes. But you listen to his entire life and you realize so many things had been done unto him; he had been abused, he had alcoholic parents, he had been on the streets himself since the time he was a teenager, all the awful things had happened to him. So you know, you can't judge this person just by this one act; I was forced to look at his entire life. And I had great sympathy for my clients—not all of them, I have to admit not every single one of them—but most of them; my sympathy went out to them. So I think Joon is in a similar situation where she sees characters and she tries to understand the larger picture of them and not judge them by this one act. She herself is not making all the right decisions for herself, either. I guess it's Joon, but it's also my personal philosophy.

You've been quoted as saying that Miles from Nowhere *is only one percent autobiographical. You did a significant amount of research on the runaway population in the United States. At the same time,* Miles from Nowhere *is a visceral reading experience, and devastatingly authentic. Where do research and imagination intersect in your writing process?*

You know everyone does their research a little differently. I think people who write historic novels do the research first and then sit down and write. I did my research more toward the latter part of the book because I didn't want it to seem like it was research-based. When the initial feverish writing slowed down, I stopped and read a lot of letters from teens who wrote sort of imaginary letters to their parents, to get their voice a little bit, just the tone. I've read a lot of essays about not just runaways, but throwaways, temporary runaways who only go away for a little bit, permanent runaways who go away for years and never come back. I also learned about male sex workers, who are very different from female sex workers, and then of course reading about exploitation of teens and homeless people in general.

I watched a lot of documentaries as well. There is a really great documentary, everyone has to see it: it's called *Children Underground*, and it's about these kids in Romania who actually live inside a subway station, and they created their own little mini-society. The youngest is eight years old, and the oldest is something like sixteen years old. It killed me the first time I saw it; I still cry every time I see it. I used to assign it to my students. It still kills me because it actually at some point takes a wider lens and sort of looks at the society and how these kids came out to be this way. So it's a much larger look at this little society.

I wanted to make sure that I didn't watch these documentaries beforehand, but I did want to make sure that I had the tone right. I mean, if you watch these documentaries and read these essays, you find there are some really funny moments that happen, like magical moments that happen in these lives. When you live in the margins, you look at and notice and are grateful for tiny moments of happiness. Those tiny little moments seem gigantic when your life is so miserable. And so I wanted to make sure that I had that tone right, that it wasn't all just going to be about despair, that there were these moments of hopefulness and beauty and tender love between these surviving, desperate characters. So that's why I did the research, mostly for the tone.

Do you remember any big breakthrough moment in revision in any of these stories?

There is a story in the book called "Avon," where Joon is selling Avon door-to-door, and she's also pregnant, and she's shooting heroin. It was a difficult subject matter to begin with because I had three big things happening. A) She's selling Avon, which is not the most typical job, so you have to really give information about how a girl like this could even get a job like that. B) She's pregnant, so I had to sort of work that into the plot and keep that thread going. C) She's still shooting heroin.

The most difficult part was that while she's selling Avon, she knocks on one particular door, which turns out to be—I know this sounds weird—the hallway confessional. This woman never opens the door, but she wants Joon to confess her sins. She has a rosary hanging out; she has a flyer that tells you all the different kind of sins, how you're supposed to do a confessional. She's basically a somewhat crazy lady living in this apartment. Joon, who is sort of feeling guilty about her situation, is put off at first, but then she comes to rely on this woman.

I just couldn't make that story work. At some point I remember telling Peter Ho Davies, my mentor at Michigan, "I want all of these things in here, but I don't think I have the writer's chops to make this work. I'm just not developed enough as a writer yet, maybe." I was just at a wall. At this point, I had revised the story for the fortieth time or something. I would try everything. I did so many bizarre things to this story. And then I sort of gave up. I thought, "Forget it. I can't make this work."

Peter gave me this advice, which I will forever take with me: He said, "You know what? You're not going to know that unless you keep trying. You've got to keep trying; you've got to keep trying."

And so I set it aside for a little bit. Luckily, I had signed up to take a playwriting class. I thought, I need to find out what's wrong with the story. I couldn't figure out how to revise it because I didn't know what the problem was. So I decided to write a play, to adapt this story to see it at a different angle. And within the first five sessions of writing this play, I knew immediately what was wrong. It was the structure. When you're writing a play there's none of those prose sentences that you're in love with, and as soon as I took away the language, I realized exactly when in the story there wasn't anything happening. It was just nice language that I'd fallen in love with, but nothing was actually happening to change the character in some way.

And then of course I went right back, as soon as I wrote the play, and incorporated the changes into my short story, and now it's one of my favorite stories. The nun character is completely different in this version because of the play. Because of the play, I had to make the nun character dramatic, otherwise she'd be boring. So the breakthrough that I had was: When you're stuck revising, try to write it in a different genre, and see what happens. Try to write it in a play, or in song lyrics, or in a poem. I realized that what happened was that I was too enamored with my own language, and I couldn't see the skeletal problems with it. And sometimes you just have to strip away that language, and be willing to just get rid of pages and pages of prose to make the story work. It's painful, but you've got to do it.

2009

ABOUT THE INTERVIEWER: **Chris Arnold** is an editor of *Telling Stories, Talking Craft*. He was assistant director of creative writing at Purdue at the time of the interview.

ZOMBIES | MOMENTS
MAKE MOVIES | THE
CEMETERY | **BENJAMIN**
ADAPTATION | **PERCY**
THE UNIVERSAL BOOK OF
MONSTERS | THE BUTCHER
KNIFE | EPIPHANIC DEW

Benjamin Percy

Moments Make Movies, Zombies, Adaptation, The Universal Book of Monsters, The Cemetery, The Butcher Knife, Epiphanic Dew

Benjamin Percy is the author of a novel, *The Wilding* (forthcoming in Fall 2010), and two books of short stories, *Refresh, Refresh* and *The Language of Elk*. His fiction and nonfiction have been read on National Public Radio, performed at Symphony Space, and published by *Esquire, Men's Journal, Paris Review, Chicago Tribune, Glimmer Train*, and others. He lives in Ames, Iowa, with his wife and two children and teaches creative writing in the MFA program at Iowa State University.

Many of your stories open with a striking image that sets the thematic tone for the rest of the story. For example, a freezer leaking blood, a mule deer tangled in a barbed wire fence, two boys boxing until bloodied. What are your primary concerns when starting a story, and how do you know when you've got it right?

There's this screenwriting term, 'MMM'—moments make movies – and the idea behind it is that if somebody's shopping around a script what a potential producer is looking for is two moments at least, maybe three, that are just visceral experiences last with the audience so that when they leave that theater and, minutes later, hours later, weeks later, years later are thinking about that movie, they remember that scene in particular.

And if you think of *Psycho* you think of the shower scene, right? The butcher-knife. It's usually a set piece moment, where—if you're familiar with that term—you know that's this elongated set-up of a scene that's sort of like a story in miniature within the larger story, so you know the shower scene with its beginning, middle and end. With its rising action, its goal interrupted the falling away from action as the blood swirls down the drain. Just think of so many other films, whether it's *Raiders of the Lost Ark* with that rolling boulder, or *The Graduate* when Dustin Hoffman is standing in the doorway not sure whether he's going to leave or not and Mrs. Robinson begins to peel off her clothes, or *Jaws* when the boat is descending into the water—Roy Schneider's balanced there with his rifle, the shark's plowing towards him. These are the moments that stick in our memory and, for me, I'm usually thinking of those moments as either the inciting incident for me—so many of my stories begin that way—or they're the climactic moment that I'm working towards all along.

If you think of 'Swans'—that's another visceral opening, and it's an image that was stuck in my own memory, that I'd been sorting of turning over and over in my hands trying to find a way to work it into a piece and it begins with these young women who are jumping off of a cliff into a lagoon, and that was drawn from my own experience when I was in sixth grade or something like that. I was floating in this lagoon with my goggles on and I discovered that I could see their bikinis torn away beneath the water so I floated there 'til my skin wrinkled over. And you know they would close their eyes and their arms were out and they looked as though they were boiling with bubbles all around them. And the deer being caught in barbed wire—that's a true story. That's another thing drawn from memory.

Your mind's a filter and things get clogged in it. And that's something that has electricity around it—something that sizzles, something that, you know, has the power to sort of grab the audience and set them on their way. So, I think beginnings and endings have to do that. Beginnings are all about sucking you in, dragging you down the rabbit hole; and endings, where you also have those impactful moments, those are all about resonance. You know, the thing that's gonna make people think about this story later on. It's still humming.

What sort of images are stuck in your filter? Do you build a story around it, or is it something you just put aside until you find the right story where you can use that image?

I've got this big bulletin board next to my desk and I tack all sorts of stuff to it so—pictures that might be clipped from magazines or I might have taken them myself, I've got snippets of dialogue that are overheard, images that I just have in my head for some reason, or anecdotes, articles clipped from newspapers—every time I sit down at my desk I glance over at it, not in an intentional way, really, but just sort of, you know, I glance at it every day, sometimes thirty times a day, when I sit down. And what happens over time is these three things rise up in a constellation and I realize that they work together.

In "The Caves of Oregon" there's this house with a cave beneath it that sort of serves as a kind of natural basement, and that's an actual house. When I was in fourth or fifth grade we were shopping around for houses and this was a neighborhood in Bend and I really wanted my parents to buy that house. And it's a good thing they didn't because later on it collapsed upon itself like the House of Usher, but from the time I was ten or eleven until the time I was, oh I don't know, twenty-six maybe, when I wrote that story, it was just lingering there, waiting. I'm not certain right away how something's going to fit together with something else. I'm not certain how I'm gonna make a story out of an idea, I just wait until it rises up, until it feels like I'm plugged in to the idea; and what I do is, usually I always know where I'm going to end a story when I begin it. I don't know all the details but I pretty much know where it's gonna end, and some people don't like that idea—like Dan Chaon, I don't know if you guys have ever had him out here before, ever read his work, but he's the author of *Among the Missing*, which is just a dynamite short story collection. He was nominated for the National Book Award for that collection of short stories and he's an organic writer. He just lets it happen, lets it flow. He writes, as a result of that, about a hundred and fifty pages for every short story; he just lays out all the pages on the floor and looks around at them and gathers them up and realizes like 'These fifteen, this is the story.' Then he rewrites it according to those fifteen, and that's great—he views writing as an act of discovery. He doesn't think writing...he doesn't want to write unless it's about discovery.

But that's a lot of work and I kind of like to know where I'm headed. I don't go down as many blind alleys as a result, I feel like there's momentum that comes from knowing where you're going 'cause every paragraph is sort of crashing into the next like a series of dominoes. If I have maybe in mind, a few scenes in the middle, just barely realized or an image in the middle and some sort of aiming through that image on my way towards that ending that's conceived.

Some of your stories forsake the Joycean epiphanic ending. They end in the middle with that immediate tension. How do you decide to end at that point, to not have that sort of epiphany that a lot of us are taught?

The epiphany sometimes feels, to me, false and tacked on. And though occasionally I want my characters to figure things out, I don't know if it would necessarily be believable when you consider some of the people I'm writing about. I mean sometimes we know more than they do, we as readers. Sometimes I feel like I don't want everything to be wrapped up sort of neatly—a finished short story is just a glimpse into a life and you come in the middle of things and you sometimes end in the middle of things instead of having that final bow on top of the neatly wrapped package. If you just think about impact, what I'm going for is the moment after a cannon fires and the air is shaking. That's how I want people to feel when they put down my stuff—feel it in their bones.

You talked about when you're writing a story, you know where the ending is and how the story goes toward that point. I'm gonna ask you about your novel, about the act of writing that, because it's such a longer project. Was it the same process for you?

I wrote three failed novels before I sold *The Wilding* and they weren't a waste of time at all, you know, I figured out a lot by writing them. In fact, I harvested a lot of what's in them to place in short stories, and even some paragraphs, some images are supplanted in the present novel. And what happened with this novel that's coming out in the fall, it wasn't ready coming out of the gates when Fiona bought it—Fiona McCrae at Graywolf Press—this is March of 2008. When she bought it she said—she has a British accent so everything she says sounds very reasonable—"This is quite good. We would love to publish it, but would you be amendable to some changes?" And I said "Sure, yeah, all right." And she said, "Well, we would like you to shift it from first person to third person and in doing so, create, with the freedom afforded to the characters, create five interlocking subplots that come to a head at once." "All right," not really realizing how much work that was, and it was exactly the right advice because what I gave to her was—it was still clinging to the short form.

It was sort of an elongated short story; it was like a 'shnovel.' And it limited—'cause it was obviously not what I was doing in the previous book. It wasn't working. I had sort of these vast casts and, you know, enormous stretches of time so it was like "All right, I'm gonna have like three characters in one place in one weekend and that's gonna be my novel." And I thought of it as kind of a transitional book as I figured out the form. After that I was like "No, no, no, no, no. That's just one plotline within the novel." And so she helped me expand that sort of world that I'd created. I rewrote the book—it took me a year, and I mostly just tossed away what was already there. It's just when you're revising sometimes that's the best move, rather than feeling shackled to sentences already composed. So I rewrote the thing in a year, handed it back to her and she said "Fantastic, but, can we cut two of these subplots, add in another female perspective and change the ending and… and…and…" "All right." So I got back to working.

So all this time I'm renovating my house, I'd just moved into a new house. So I'm ripping off wallpaper, and mudding walls—texturing and painting, and ripping out outlets, and putting in new light fixtures and ripping out carpets, and refinishing floors. It became a perfect metaphor for what I was doing with this book. So I got back to work—this was, again, March-April a year later—so I revise according to her wishes and it was like October. I handed her the draft and she said "Yes, now you got it."

So it didn't come easily, and in part it has to do with realizing a novel is a different sort of animal. It's not just a longer story. It has to do with language, and your language can't be as intense as it is in a short story or you're gonna exhaust your audience. You know, a novel is a bit messier—there's not quite as much precision. You know, you have to allow yourself the opportunity to digress. Sometimes the best stuff comes out of those digressions. It also has to do with just the way you structure.

When I was in grad school I was very diligent about having a notebook next to me, a yellow legal table next to me, and I tried to figure out how stories were put together. So I'd have a Flannery O'Connor story and I'd read it five times so I'd be emotionally detached from the work, and then I'd start to map it out: Paragraph one, character A, character B, scene, ending is hinted at, trope number one introduced...so I had like this diagram and I had another story and I'd try to use that same skeleton. You'd never recognize it as the same work but it's different flesh on the same skeleton. Then I started to do the same thing with Tim O'Brien. Tim O'Brien is a completely different writer from Flannery O'Connor—he's got this elliptical style where he's juggling images. He's juggling objects so he's got, sort of, all these balls up in the air and he's going like this...and, you know, that became sort of the style I told all of my stories in if you look at "Caves in Oregon" or you look at "Refresh, Refresh." That's how those stories were, you know, I've got about twelve different tropes that I'm cycling back through and they're swelling in power and meaning and then they all come crashing down in the final scene. That doesn't work necessarily in a novel, you can't do that elliptical thing necessarily in a three hundred page expanse 'cause there's not enough momentum to it—there's not enough pull. You need causality in a novel, you need one thing leading to another thing so that there's that want to follow these characters for the next three weeks or four weeks.

A lot of your short stories use section breaks, where in some cases the sections are only a page, two pages and others are six to seven. Is this something where you know, in revision, you want these sections to be short and so you find a way to put it in that space, or do the sections just occur organically for you?

Well organically, you know, they're commercial breaks. The tension rises and there's moments where you want your audience to gasp or to laugh, or you want some image to be particularly memorable to them, or you want to say "This is important—this line of dialogue." So you cut away right then and there's only the white space for them to float through and say "Oh..." And if the scene had kept going, it wouldn't have been as powerful, necessarily, if you had tried to create the transitions, the ligature, it might be all snarled up.

So within each of those sections, typically what I'm doing is introducing or reintroducing two or three tropes. So, if you just think of maybe the more obvious example of "Refresh, Refresh," you know, you'll have in the opening section the circle of dirt in the yard with the hose that's set up as the fighting ring. And that ring reappears—it's almost like a math formula, you know: two pages later, two pages later, two pages later. And the ring—the grass begins to scrape away. The ring becomes more shallow—it becomes recessed. It begins to take on the look of scabbed flesh...and it directly echoes the crater, a hole in the ground. Which itself echoes a kind of war-torn territory we might imagine from one of the other tropes. You know, you've got these meteors, these shooting stars that are flying through the night sky that are directly associated with tracer rounds. And you have, in addition to a meteor coming down from the sky and opening up the earth, you have peregrine falcons swooping down and seizing up a chip to carry off to some invisible place to feast upon. And you have the war swooping down to carry off these fathers. And you have other tropes like the way steam or smoke is used all throughout the story. So, they're—steam's blasting from their mouths as they're fighting, they're boiling over; and smoking cigarettes when they stand over Dave Leidner, the recruitment officer, after they've beaten him; smoking cigarettes after they've killed the deer; the tailpipe of their dirt bike smokes...So I've got about ten other things that I've sort of got floating around there and they're contained within these units they've got these little corrals within those section breaks.

Your stories in general do not shy away from the political climate. They're also very much set in an area—in your case the high desert in Oregon. Can you talk a little about how setting impacts your work?

That political element is something I've thought a lot about. I feel like it's important to address political issues, it's important to be relevant and timely in what you're hammering about. The danger, I think, is in when you get too partisan, when you get a little too editorial. I try to make every effort to just kind of tow a line so that it's not necessarily evident to my audience how I feel about the war. The boys feel pride for their fathers even as they feel resent for the conflict. I think it's something that's worth talking about. I worry when fiction feels like an afterschool special—when it feels like there's some sort of message, when it feels like an editorial. I more want my audience to sort of think about the issue than think about what I think. So to make them feel, to make them experience something.

Regarding setting, that's essential to me. I think of setting as a character—and I mean that in a few different ways. I think of setting as a character in that I try to bend the world around the point-of-view of my character; so, they see the world in a particular place. It's seen through the lens of their character. Think of Julian in "Everything That Rises Must Converge," a Flannery O'Connor story. He steps out of the house, and what does he see? A sunset that he describes as a dying violet. Who thinks of sunsets that way? Sunsets bring out the romance in us—he sees it as a dying violet, you already understand something about it. Then he looks around further and the houses in the neighborhood, he sees them as bulbous, liver-colored monstrosities. Isn't that the greatest adjective ever? Liver-colored? And then around each house there's "a narrow collar of dirt in which sat, usually, a grubby child." But the mother sees the world in a completely different place—his mother, but, we're not aligned with her point of view, we're with Julian.

So I try to think of it that way, but also in terms of setting as a character, setting rising up to inform a scene so that a sunset or, you know, the way a tree sort of shakes against the wind, or anything else, you know, the shadows thrown by the mountains...That's informing the scene in the same way that a character might, the way a character's line of dialogue or a character's gesture might.

I talk about this a lot with my students in trying to figure out their own backyard and what's interesting about it, what're the myths that you grew up with? What about the landscape deserves your attention? And a lot of people will say, "Well, nothing. Where I grew up is boring." And you just make them look a little closer. So, maybe they grew up in a small town in Iowa where there's 400 people. That in itself is interesting, like maybe it's just off the interstate and the only reason people stop there is to get gas. Well then, play around with that. Like, maybe there's that constant—maybe the characters constantly are looking to the horizon thinking that something better is waiting for them there. Maybe isolation is an important theme to play around with in this landscape. What about the way those corn rows march off in to the distance or the way the clouds pile up like mountains or the way that that slaughterhouse that's twenty miles down the round, you know, how a fog of kind of rancid meat stink hangs over the town when the wind blows right? All these things help create atmosphere and uniqueness.

I'm curious about something you wrote this in a review of a Stephen King novel: "The best horror stories take a knife to the anxieties of the time." What do you see as the anxieties of our time being? And what can literary writers learn from horror, other genres, and vice versa?

What I was talking about was the way that books like Frankenstein are born out of Industrial Revolution. The way that Dracula is born out of Victorian prudishness. If you look at all those alien invasion movies that came out during, ah, the Red Scare. If you look at Stephen King's career, and the way he's constantly reinvented himself to sort of match what's going on in the world and what we're worried about. You've got the bio-terror of *The Stand*, and you have the industrial horrors of "Graveyard Shift." And you have books like his latest, *Under the Dome*, which is his first and one of the first, I feel like, post 9-11 horror novels.

You can track this through the movies as well if you're looking. You know, George Romero is a fitting example. Each one of his dead movies, from the Living Dead series, each one of them reinvents itself so you have Night of the Living Dead coming out of the civil rights movement. You have Dawn of the Dead—the rise of consumerism, takes place in a mall, you can't tell the zombies from the mannequins from the people. His latest one had to do with media and how these people were recording sort of Blair Witch style, zombies all around them in sort of an entertaining fashion. You know it's happening in this was that's sort of like Big Brother's always watching around us.

I think it's important even if you're not writing horror to realize the moment that you're in. I had somebody once ask me why I wrote about the war when I hadn't served myself, and there's some sort of distrust there, I guess. And my feeling was, how can you not write about the war in some capacity? How can you not write about the anxieties of this time? Even if not directly, Iraq or Afghanistan or something else should somehow cast its shadow over your work. Barry Lopez once said that as writers, we're servants of memory. So if you think about the fact that—I don't know—look at the newspapers, and on the front page you've got news of Paris Hilton and Tiger Woods, and then buried on page eight, you've got some headline—you know, tucked into the corner—about fifteen people, fifteen soldiers dying in Afghanistan. And that's wrong, so, it's an effort to sort of bully these issues into people's heads again.

When it comes to horror it's just a genre that for me has been important since childhood. I can remember that moment when I went into the library in kindergarten and I pulled off the shelf the *Universal Book of Monsters* and I opened up the page to the Wolfman. He's got this hoggish nose and shag-carpeting hair and it really bothered me; I was scared shitless for the rest of the day and through the night, I was crying. And then the next day I went back to the library and pulled it off the shelf again. I'm interested in a way that—well, there's a certain joy in writing in that genre, and I think there's also something to be studied in the way that a lot of writers these days are straddling genres. They're taking all the skills they learned from literary fiction: characterization—rounded characterization, careful carpentry of language, stunning metaphors—taking all of that good stuff and then applying it to some of the archetypes of genre, some of the beats of genre. Look at Karen Russell, look at Dan Chaon, look at Kevin Brockmeier, look at Margaret Attwood, look at Dan Simmons. And their writing is top drawer—Michael Chabon, Jonathan Lethem. And what they're doing is a kind of slipstream thing—it's neither fish nor fowl, right? I mean the bad thing about literary fiction is sometimes nothing happens, and it ends sparkling with epiphanic dew, all right? And then the bad thing about genre fiction is that sometimes the characters are cardboard cutouts you can punch a fist through, and the language is transparent. You blend them together and it can have exciting results.

Can you speak more about the genres that you're playing with?

If you look at *Refresh, Refresh* as an example, the collection, you've got "Caves in Oregon," that's a haunted house story. There's no ghosts, but it's a haunted house story. You look at "Meltdown" and some people might refer to that as sci-fi in the way that a melt—a nuclear meltdown—results in a sort of lawless territory in the Pacific Northwest, but I was thinking more of a Western actually. I wanted to write a Western. I wanted to write a contemporary Western, but I couldn't figure out how to make this place lawless, in fact, where all these bad things could happen, and where we could have this person who's trying to bring order to the place. So instead of, you know, I threw in the sort of politicized nuclear meltdown, and then instead of having him on a white horse, instead he's riding into town on a Harley. And you have a bunch of bandits roaming around. And instead of having the schoolmarm with the heart of gold, you have, ah, a young girl who helps him find the straight and narrow. And, "Crash," one of the later stories in the book, that's a ghost story. "The Killing" is a revenge story.

I love pulp comics and pulp books from the forties and fifties, and I just was like, "I'm gonna write a revenge story." So I studied up and there it was. I'm just toying around with the same thing that Sergio Leone's toying around with. The opening of *The Good, The Bad and The Ugly* sort of exemplifies my vision in a way. It opens up with the hero—I mean not a hero, a rider coming into town—and it's high noon, and there's a guy on the other side of town and they start to walk towards each other and pull aside their coats and there's a tumbleweed and a mangy dog and there's this creaky boardwalk, and all those things that you expect—dust—from Westerns. And instead of doing what you think they're gonna do, which is pull out their six-shooters and fire, they end up being in cahoots and they turn in to the saloon and fire together at the character known as The Ugly, who then fires them and kills them. He busts out the window with a big hunk of meat in his hand, strings of turkey between his teeth, a sort of sinister mustache, and he rides off into the distance as these guys die on the floor of the saloon. It's great, I love that. I love how he takes the conventions of the Western genre and he snaps them over his knee—you know, attempting to reinvent the wheel.

You've written a lot of nonfiction now—you write for Esquire sometimes and you have a piece in the Paris Review—can you talk some about, as a fiction writer, what you see as important to know if you're trying to tackle nonfiction?

I was kind of uninterested in non-fiction—I tried out a few pieces and they ended unsuccessfully. But then, through my relationship with *Esquire,* I was assigned projects and would write them out of economic interest and because the subjects were intriguing to me. And I just basically tried out for the first time—in earnest—what I had known all along, and that's that the tricks of fiction are the tricks of creative nonfiction. I've actually fallen in love with the form in a way, and I've been writing quite a bit of nonfiction lately—craft essays that have been appearing in *Poets & Writers* and will continue to appear there as I'm working on a book of craft ideas, and also these personal essays that have been cropping up in different places like *Orion* and *Paris Review* and *Esquire.*

So, for me, it's about constantly being energized at the keyboard, and I don't know if you've ever felt this way or not, but you bust out twenty short stories and then maybe you feel like you need something new to play around with so you maybe wrestle with that bear of a novel for a while and then you get tired of that so you jump in to essays and then you get tired of that so you play around with a screenplay and then you get tired of that so you go to comics—you know, you pitch a comic series—and then you get a little tired of that so you jump back to short stories again. So that's what I do, and as a result I've never had writer's block, 'cause I just code-shift whenever I feel like things are getting stale.

How do tropes and motifs come to you? How do they emerge?

I definitely don't set out in a story thinking "Well, this orange, a pack of gum, and um…the color blue will be meaningful when repeated in this piece. It connects more to the way I revise, I suppose, in that I don't bust something out and then go back and overhaul it. Instead every time I sit down for the day I begin editing what I've already written; so if I'm talking about a short story, I mean, obviously, from the first line forward—with a novel from the beginning of a chapter I'm working on forward. So I might spend three hours in revision mode or editing mode before I'm producing new imaginative work. So, as I do that—constantly going over and going over and going over something—I'm realizing these things that maybe stand out, that maybe are pulsing. So there's oh, maybe I've got water in this story, and I wonder what that means…and it's in this other scene that I wrote. I start to realize that maybe the last scene has to take place at the lake, or that this idea of cleansing, or this idea of inheritance, or whatever else. It begins organically, and these things just rise up and announce themselves as being important. So, I might refine a story, I might revise a story twenty times, thirty times and I still won't be finished with it; so by the time I get to that final period, it's done, and that's the way that the tropes call themselves to attention.

Charles Baxter writes about the subject in *Burning Down the House*—I don't know if you've ever picked up the book or not—he calls it rhyming action and he uses the example of Lolita. She's always talking through her bubblegum, yeah, so she's got these half-formed sentences as she's smacking her gum like "Gee, gosh," and it comes to represent her innocence, and by the time you get to the end of the book you've got that great scene where Humbert Humbert (whose name is a rhyme itself—his name is a double), he comes in to the paper manor where Clare Quilty lives with Lolita, and Clare Quilty has consumed just about everything there is to consume from Lolita at this point. And Humbert blasts, I mean he pulls out his gun and shoots and there's this bloody progression down the hallway and Clare Quilty falls back onto his bed and as he's laying there this big bubble of blood—with juvenile connotations—comes out of his mouth and bursts. The idea is that he's consumed Lolita—that she's inside him and has gone through adolescence and emerged bloody. And Charles Baxter talks about how he thinks that the best tropes, the best rhymes, the best echoes, whatever you want to call it, that they're subtle—that they're there for the reader who wants to look twice, but your everyday reader's just gonna slide right over them and that's the way most metaphors—the best metaphors—should work.

A wise old man named Roger Ebert once said that the great thing about the overlying metaphor in *One Flew Over the Cuckoo's Nest*—and this applies to any story, I think—is that you can watch it, and you can enjoy the hell out of it, and still get something out of it, and not realize that, you know, this mental hospital is a metaphor for society. So that's how my tropes are functioning as well, I think.

How do you integrate research into work? A lot of your characters have interesting jobs, and almost all your characters have jobs—memorable ones—and you're really convincing about how they do their jobs. We never doubt it.

Research is essential to fiction, and in fact, I always assign research to my students in my fiction workshops, and it oftentimes is born out of a job. So the job is they're in the service or the job is they're taxidermists or the job is they work in a foundry. I think it's important to bend the world around the gig. So, if you look at Kevin McIlvoy's "The People Who Own Pianos," everything to his character, who is a piano mover, everything is a tight hallway or a narrow staircase. Everything in the world is divided into the people who own pianos and the people who don't.

And in that same way let's say you were writing a story about fashion model—something really caricatured and stereotypical because those are the best examples. She walks into a room and we're aligned with her point of view, what does she see? Maybe she looks for a reflective surface to check herself out in, maybe she compares herself to others in the room, maybe she looks at the paint splashed on the walls and wonders if it contrasts with her outfit. I don't know, but you see bending the world around that. In the same way really trying to dive in to all this research, to really understand the world that these people live in, you know the terminology, the language they employ. The way that they might view a relationship. The way they might deal with their emotions can be informed by the job that they have.

So in the example of "Caves in Oregon" the guy works at a foundry. And that's something that I tumbled upon as a news junkie—I'm always flipping through magazines and newspapers, listening to NPR, surfing the net—and I came across this article about a guy who worked in a foundry and there was a picture of him with a fifty pound sledgehammer and in the background there's all this molten ore—it was like Mordor, you know. And this was his life, he was underground all day smashing things and he was covered in soot. And I was like "Wow, it's the underground man." So I clipped it out and it sat—I've got a folder in my desk of story ideas—eventually it got tacked up on the bulletin board. I went and visited a foundry, I got on the phone with a few people, I did some research through the electronic archives—always a great treasure to have for any university you might work for, and I learned all there is to learn about alloys and smashing things with a sledgehammer and, uh, it comes to partner all sorts of other things in the story: the fact that they're retreating underground as they sort of get through their grief, the fact that he's swinging the pain out of his system.

If you look at the taxidermist story and "The Killing," you know, the relationship in that case is pretty obvious where you've got this guy who's gonna take somebody out and he's surrounded by the dead. But you know, more than that it has to do with credibility, convincing us of this world. So I've got to categorize all the polyurethane forms and glass eyeballs that he uses in his shop and the formaldehyde that he reeks of.

We spend most of our lives working. What I notice about most stories is they forget about that—they forget that their characters have jobs. When we spend most of our lives at the desk or in line at the factory or driving back and forth between the time we punch in and punch out. So work, to me, is essential, and it's typical of the research component that comes in.

You were talking earlier about harvesting previous works and then supplanting that in current work. I'm curious about two stories—the first one's an early story, "The Whale" and the other story's "When the Bear Came Down" The earlier story seems to inform the later story.

I created a cemetery folder on my computer. So in the cemetery folder I've got lots of headstones, lots of folders within that folder: images, characters, first lines, it goes on and on. I've found that it's so much easier to cut—to kill your darlings, to take them out to pasture and shoot them in the head—when there's a cemetery for them. Because you know how it is when you've got fourteen drafts of the same piece—by the time you get to that fourteenth you can't remember what was in draft three, it's gone. That makes it that much harder to cut, to change things.

If you've got a cemetery folder, you pluck them you drop them in their plot, then there's that possibility—and this is mostly psychological—but there's always that possibility that you can go back there and you can bring down the lightning and you can do a voodoo dance and they'll rise up again. That sometimes happens. I'll be writing a story and I'll think to myself, don't I have some description of mountains that got from a story? Description of mountains...yes! Or didn't I have something in here about like a domestic fight, some sort of domestic argument that's just dialogue, there's no context for it? Oh yeah, there it is. More often, the stuff just rots, but it's helpful, you know, to learn, in part, because I feel like nothing is wasted, and I mean that not only in writing things that will never see the light of day, but I figure out something through their composition. Also in the way that from the past I've taken dead stories and harvested organs and bones from them.

My graduate thesis was a novel. I wrote a book of short stories while I was there but my thesis was a novel. So, *Language of Elk*, I wrote that while I was there—most of those stories were written when I was 23, 24. But then I, as a challenge, I wanted to try writing a novel. I had the time in grad school, so I wrote this really crappy book called *King of the Wild Frontier*, and I ended up using bits and pieces—like the fight scenes in "Refresh, Refresh"—directly lifted from that novel. Couldn't be a more different context though. The elk in "The Language of Elk," that short story, that's directly lifted from that book. And other things, like the character in the woods, the character of the father in the woods, comes directly out of that manuscript.

Other writers are like this as well. Lorrie Moore—I've heard that she wastes nothing, like even sentences, she won't let them go, she'll find some other way to fit them in at a later date. And with those stories in particular—you're talking about "The Whale" and "When the Bear Came"—and I've got another one as well that some people have referred to—"The Hand" and "The Long, Black Coat." Reading Carver, I was really interested in the way that he came back to stories later and refinished them. He wasn't satisfied with them, and part of that was because of the influence of [Gordon] Lish and how he felt like sometimes his vision had been sort of skewed—that his stories had been hijacked—and so he wanted them to be published the way he wanted them. It was also just that he wasn't quite satisfied with the way the language was or the way the characters were developed. So you look at *Where I'm Calling From*, right? And then you look at those same stories in some of the other collections, "The Bath" and "A Small Good Thing." "The Bath" is the classic Lish version—it's very sinister and it ends and you know, you wanna go walk in front of a bus. "A Small Good Thing" is a very hopeful story—not to mention a longer one, the sentences even are more muscular.

So with "The Whale" I was reading "Butcher Boy" at the time by Patrick McCabe so I actually had that voice in my head, and I just felt like the language was a little bit sloppy. I started off like many writers writing in the first person and sort of doing mimicry, doing something theatrical where "Hey I'm this character and I'm doing a song and dance like them." And later on what happened was I sort of transitioned into third, and you know, sort of had my own voice—the puppet master voice—and I like the control of that. Even as I align the point of view with my character I still have my voice controlling it, and so I went back to the story, and I sort of took the structure of it and the vision of it and altered the voice completely and made it more like the voice I have now instead of the twelve-year-old boy, the sort of ranting, lyrical, crass voice.

So I changed the voice and then I changed the context. You know the original context is—this is a true story from Oregon you probably know about—this whale washed up on shore and they didn't know how to get rid of it. It was rotting, stinking up the beach. They shoved it full of dynamite and blew it up—go to YouTube, you can see the video. You know, this was one of those myths that I grew up with in Oregon, so I had to write about that. But then I, I don't know, it just started to linger with me and out of dissatisfaction I put it in a new context, and it was also due to the fact that I wanted to have that story—the heart of that story—in my collection. And a coast story wouldn't work. I wanted it to be in the high desert. So a new landscape as well. The whale becomes a bear.

2010

ABOUT THE INTERVIEWER: **James Xiao** was fiction editor for *Sycamore Review* at the time of the interview. He earned his MFA in creative writing from Purdue University.

SCREENWRITING | SHIFTLESS PEOPLE | SOUTHERN GOTHIC | **STEVE** REJECTION | **YARBROUGH** THE TRAPPINGS OF DAY-TO-DAY LIFE | MISTAKES | MASCULINE AUTHORITY

Steve Yarbrough

Rejection, Masculine Authority, Southern Gothic, The Trappings of Day-to-Day Life, Mistakes, Shiftless People, Screenwriting

Born in Indianola, Mississippi, Steve Yarbrough is the author of five novels: *Safe from the Neighbors*, *The End of California*, *Prisoners of War*, *Visible Spirits* and *The Oxygen Man*. He has also written several short story collections. A PEN/Faulkner finalist, he has received the Mississippi Authors Award, the California Book Award, the Richard Wright Award, and an award from the Mississippi Institute of Arts and Letters. He now teaches at Emerson College and lives with his wife in Stoneham, Massachusetts.

In The Oxygen Man, *you use a pattern of interwoven narrative threads covering two characters, Ned and Daisy "Daze" Rose, and two time periods, 1996 and 1972-3. The jumps you make between characters and time periods, and the juxtapositions you create, are quite effective and produce a lot of dramatic tension. It calls to mind the use of "jump cuts" in film. I know you wrote a screenplay for* The Oxygen Man *before completing the novel. Did writing the screenplay inform your final revisions?*

It wasn't the writing of the screenplay itself that made me go back to the novel with a different eye. It was thinking about the characters again after not having been involved with them for a couple of years, because that's when I got asked to do the screenplay. The novel had been out there for about two years at that time. I think I've just always written cinematically. It's just what comes naturally to me. When I have to write a paragraph saying what something looks like, or when I have to write a paragraph with only one character in it, where he's walking downtown or something like that, that's where writing gets hard for me. If I've got two or more characters in a concrete environment, speaking to one another and doing things, that's easy writing for me. So, I think that's just the way that I write fiction, especially in the novels. Less so in some of my later short stories that are first person because I think those are more voice-driven than the novel and some of the third-person stories.

The paradox of Ned Rose's end in The Oxygen Man *is really terrific and powerful—it is both "a failure of sorts," to borrow Ned's own phrase, and terrifically liberating both for himself and for his sister. At what point in the drafting process did this conclusion present itself or was it the plan from the very beginning?*

I had a plan for that ending from the beginning. In the original version of the novel, we ended with the scene between Ned and Mack in the pickup truck, and then there was a tiny coda that actually had a lot in common with what became the prologue in the book. It was a dreamlike coda that got a little bit too self-conscious, sort of suggesting what might lie in wait for Ned down the road. And so when I rewrote it, it really struck me that that didn't work, and that what we needed to do was go back to the sister at the very end. All five of the sections begin with the sister. It seemed to me that what was appropriate for the novel was to end with the sister. In the earliest version of the novel, Daze and Ned never really came to terms with one another at all. She hated him right to the last word of the book. The book is dark, anyway, but that was an absolutely black-hearted look at those two characters.

When you finish a novel, you're usually a different person than when you started. That's not true with stories. After I'd let a couple of years go by, and that novel had been rejected everywhere, and I thought about it, I realized I didn't feel the same way about those characters as I had when I'd started. One of the things that was wrong with the book, and I think one of the reasons why nobody would publish the book, was that the central relationship in the story remained static all the way through. There's not a hell of a lot of movement now, but there's a lot more than there was in the beginning.

At the end of your story "The Atlas Bone" you have a really provocative paragraph on the topic of fathers and sons. In it, your narrator says that "fathers are everywhere among us and in this life you can never escape them, because when you leave one behind, another will turn up. In the end we ourselves become the fathers, and so there is not and cannot be among men such a thing as brotherhood, only fatherhood and sonhood, and the only just act is to annihilate the father in ourselves." Isn't this, in part, what motivates Ned Rose to turn against Mack Bell in The Oxygen Man?

Yeah, in a sense, I think he's turning against a figure of male authority, or masculine authority of a particular kind. Because I think Beer Smith represents a different kind of masculine authority—a kind that I feel drawn to. But I don't feel drawn to the other kind. In the story you mentioned, "The Atlas Bone," if you look at the masculine authority that those two characters are both, in their own ways, in rebellion against, well, one of them is a military man who is used to issuing commands and just having them be accepted. The other one, the doctor, is in some sense very militaristic himself.

I think if you look at Ned's father—not taking him, at least, from this vantage point—this is somebody who has completely abdicated any kind of authority, any kind of fathering. The closest he ever comes to it is when they take that ride in the pickup truck together. In the end, there's not much they can say to each other.

You mentioned Beer Smith. He's been a character in your fiction from Family Men *up to* The Oxygen Man. *He is a figure of compassion and generosity, a catalyst, a man who offers people chances to start over. I think of him as a kind of "moral center" to your work. You've written about him so many times, I have to ask: what is it that attracts you to him?*

Well, let me ask myself a question, first, that you didn't ask me: Is he based on anybody you knew growing up? And he's not. I think he's a representation of what I didn't know growing up, or the person I didn't know growing up. It seems to me that he's a guy who has put more back into the world than he's ever tried to take from it. I wish there were more people around like that. I wish I was more like that, or could be. I think the closest thing that I ever saw to Beer Smith was my maternal grandfather, who was in many ways that sort of person, who did his best to give a little back to the world.

For me, he [Beer Smith] is the moral center of that town. And at the same time, because of what he does in his business, which is to sell booze, he will always be a little bit of an outsider in a Bible Belt town.

1 really admire Ned's dreamlike prologue to The Oxygen Man. *A similar moment occurs in that chilling paragraph following the fight between Ned and Mack in the car in 1913, when Ned thinks he hears the spirit of a slave howling. Literally and figuratively, Ned is haunted by ghosts. And, to be certain, the atmosphere of the novel is permeated with its share of gloom and anxiety. Is this the long-hallowed "Southern gothic" creeping into Steve Yarbrough's work?*

Oh, I don't know. I'm not sure I've ever understood the term "Southern gothic." I come out of a culture in which ghosts are, in some basic way, real. It doesn't mean I ever saw one. But if you're thinking about something that is, in the corporeal sense, not there, but you're thinking about it to the extent that it becomes a fact for you, well, then, is it real? I'm tempted to say it's the most real thing of all, that the things that are most real are not the ones that are out there that we can look at and understand. They're these things that we fear all the time. So, if that's a peculiarly Southern trait—and it may be, I don't know—I suppose we could say, yes, the Southern gothic is creeping in.

Richard Ford gave a talk at Purdue University a couple of years ago in which he discussed the question of a writer's origins. Ford was born in Jackson, Mississippi, but he says that he has never considered himself a "Southern writer." Rather, he is a writer from the South. Do you consider yourself a Southern writer? Do labels like that mean anything to you?

I don't think most writers like an adjective put before the word "writer." On the one hand, it's a label I could wear proudly enough. It's a great tradition to come out of. On the other hand, I think anything that gets stuck onto the front of the word "writer" like that has an amazing capacity to limit what you can do, or what you think you can do. I don't write exclusively about the south. At the same time, the novel I've just finished is set in Mississippi. The one I'm about to begin is going to be set in Mississippi. So, I don't know. I can imagine myself someday writing a novel set in Poland. I've written a good bit about Poland, and I feel it triggers my imagination in a way. But I would hate to think that, because of where I come from, what I'm going to be allowed to write about is in any way limited. In the end, I'll decide what I write about. So I suppose I would agree with Richard. I think of myself as a writer from the South.

Place is of central importance to you as a writer. Most of your fiction centers on your home town of Indianola, Mississippi. What is it about that place, and about place in general, that calls you as a writer?

I guess I just know it so well. I can lay my hands on details very easily. Since I'm a traditional, realistic writer, I really need the trappings of day-to-day life. And I know the trappings of day-to-day life in that place very well. Something that's a little more mysterious to me is what is it about Poland that makes me keep going back and writing about it? I have conflicted feelings about Poland. I love it, and if you say anything bad about it I'll argue with you. On the other hand, there are things about it that are just utterly exasperating to me. That's one thing that's common, I guess, about my perceptions of Poland and my perceptions of the Mississippi Delta. But Fresno, where I've lived for twelve years, I almost never feel drawn to write about. I have written about it a couple of times, but even though that's my day-to-day reality, it's never really triggered my imagination very much. So I'm not sure I can give you a real smart answer about this. I think that when you find writers who become attached to a place, so that they want to spend a large part of their lives writing about it, sometimes it's easy to figure out. With Indianola, well, it's my home. But Fresno is also my home, and it's my children's home. Yet I don't feel much drawn to it as a place to set fiction.

How have people in Indianola and the Delta in general reacted to your writing? Do they see themselves in your work? Do you want them to?

I don't want them to see themselves in my work because nobody real is in my work. I had somebody once tell me, "I know who that character was." And the character truly was not based on anybody. I said, "What do you mean?" He said, "I know who that was." And he told me who he thought it was. And I said, "Where do you get that from?" He said, "Because he's over six feet tall and his name starts with R." But it's the farthest thing from my mind. People are always going to think that they see things.

At the same time, I've never had anybody tell me that they were offended by anything that was there. Which doesn't mean there's not somebody out there who is, but if there is I've had the good fortune never to come across them.

Over the course of four books, you have drawn a vivid and memorable portrait of Sunflower County, Mississippi. I feel like if I were to go down there, I could find my way to the Piggly Wiggly, or to the Beer Smith Lounge. I could even drive over to Lee's in Greenville for a big steak. Is your fiction, like Joyce's Dubliners, *an accurate map to the geography of the area? How much artistic license have you taken with your place material?*

Well, in Indianola, Mississippi there is no Piggly Wiggly. There is no Beer Smith lounge. And in Greenville, Mississippi to the best of my knowledge, there is no Lee's Steak House. There was a Piggly Wiggly at one time, and it was right downtown on Front Street. So, no, it's not an accurate map in the geographical sense. But in another sense, I'd like to think that I've probably captured the spirit and the flavor of the place. But, no, you'd just get lost if you tried to walk around and find things.

So you definitely feel, as a writer, that you have the license to rewrite it, if you will.

Yeah. I tell people that fiction is not what did happen; fiction is what didn't happen. I had somebody once come up and tell me, "You know, you've been away a long time. You've forgotten what the school colors of Indianola Academy are. They're blue and white. They're not red and gray." And I said, "No, I know perfectly well what the colors were. But that's the real Indianola Academy, and this is the fictional one, and I can do whatever I want to with it."

At one point in your essay "Preacher," you discuss a gap that grew between you and certain members of your family, most markedly your parents and your grandmother. This gap, you write, "would eventually make me leave the place where I'd grown up and turn me into the most peculiar species of outsider: the one who can close his eyes and walk around a place without ever stumbling, guided by sound and smell, by the feel of the dirt beneath his feet." Looking back, was that gap inevitable? Was this gap necessary for you, as a writer, in order to write about Indianola?

Yeah, I think it probably was. You know, literary history is littered with stories of writers who had to become outsiders. You mentioned Joyce, who in the very literal sense became an outsider. I think I'm right in saying that for the last half of his life or so he was never in Dublin. The Polish poet Adam Mickiewicz—who is considered Poland's most important writer—after the age of about nineteen or twenty, I think, never set foot in Poland ever again. He lived in exile. And something about being gone from a place, oddly enough, for me at least, brings the place into focus.

I wrote a story once, it's in *Mississippi History*, a story called "Stay Gone Days." I never felt closer to the place I came from than when I was writing that story. Now, I was writing that story in the attic of an apartment building in Torun, Poland -just a couple streets away from the house where Copernicus grew up. I could actually see it out of the window. Roman Ingarden's son lived in the apartment down below. So, I was surrounded by things that would seem to be absolutely a world away from what I was trying to write about. But something about being so far gone from it just seemed to strengthen my imagination.

Did you ever write about Indianola while you lived there or did all the writing take place after you'd left?

I wasn't living in Indianola at this time, but three short stories from my first book were actually written in Indianola. "Family Men" was written there. "The Lode Sentry" was written there. That was when I was in graduate school and I was at home visiting. Those two stories were actually written three days apart. And then in the summer of '88, we were getting ready to move to California from North Carolina and we were broke. So we went and stayed at my parents' house for a couple of months. And I wrote the last story in *Family Men* there—I mean the last story that I wrote for the book, which was one called "Three Cheers for Ellis Fuller." So I wrote it in Indianola.

I attempted writing there at various times when I was a kid. I tried writing poetry and songs and, you know, they weren't any good. [laughs] Until recently, this year, living back in Oxford, almost everything I've written was not written in Mississippi.

I'd like to ask about the oblique endings in some of your fiction. The sense of resolution in stories like "Lady Luck" and "Rottweiler," both from Veneer, *is loose in ways that are both intriguing and exciting. The same is true, of course, of* The Oxygen Man. *What is it that attracts you to these open-ended, oblique conclusions?*

I'm not sure. There aren't many things in this world that I really feel very certain about. I don't know when I'm going to die. I don't know where I'll be in ten years, or five years, or even one year. And, I guess at some point I began to ask myself, "Well, do things really have to be spelled out that clearly in fiction?"

It's been kind of curious. I've talked to a couple of film people that have been interested in trying to free up the film rights to *The Oxygen Man.* I remember having a conversation with one person who said, "What happens at the end?" And I said, "Well, you know, what happens is what happens." And I went ahead and took the words out of her mouth and said, "But I know you can't do that in film."

Well, you can and you can't. We talked last night about the John Sayles film *Limbo,* which is as indeterminate an ending as anything I can imagine. It's just how brassy and how courageous and how unconventional are you willing to be? And most film people, at least in this country, are not willing to go that far. So, I don't know.

Of course, I've been criticized for it from time to time. But, that's just the way I write. I've been asked a lot in the last year, "What happened to him [Ned]?" And, after a while, I began to say, "Okay, here's what I think happens." And, of course, a couple people have said, "What do you mean 'think'? You wrote the book, right?"

In several of the stories in Veneer *there is a metafictional awareness of the act of constructing narrative. That is, the process of narration and composition becomes foregrounded in the story-becomes part of the story. What attracts you to the metafictional aspects of story writing?*

I'm not sure. I think if you look at the careers of short story writers at a certain point--usually near the ends of their careers, and I hope that I'm not getting there--you find they often begin to push at the boundaries of the genre. As if suddenly it becomes too small for them. That's when a lot of them turn into novelists—sometimes bad novelists. But if you look at, say, Alice Munro as a case in point, with the stories in *Open Secrets,* when she begins to use different methods of narration-newspaper excerpts, stories that circle back on themselves and also if you look at John Cheever's later stories, you see some of the same, as you put it, metafictional awareness.

I'm not sure why that happened to me writing this book. It may be that by the time I was writing this book, I had been with my wife for quite a few years, so she had heard all of my stories a kajillion times. And I remember several times at parties I would start to tell a story and she would say, "No no, that's not the way it happened." And I found myself thinking, How did it happen? I don't know. I mean, it happened the way I'm telling it at a given moment, and I'm not telling it the same way. So I think I began to think a lot more about the effects of different methods of narration. And also [I began] to become aware that it's very difficult to nail things down and say how they *did* happen. So, some of those thoughts, I think, probably had been running through my mind for some years.

I'd like to ask you about the switch from the short story to the novel, and how they cross-inform one another. Has writing a novel changed your thoughts or sense of the short form, or vice-versa?

Well, I really do feel that it's very different. I think stories have much more in common with poems than they do with novels, because, as in a poem, you've got to be able to suggest much more than you can ever say in a short story. You can't accumulate detail, you can't draw on fact to the extent that you can in a novel. And I think that makes a story incredibly difficult to master. The more I think about short stories, the more awed I am by the form itself. I think novels allow you mistakes that you can still recover from. But the story's pretty damn unforgiving.

Wallace Stegner once said that the short story was a young writer's form, and that a writer will "grow into" the novel. Does that ring true for you?

I think that rings true for certain people. Maybe I'm at that point in my life where it's happening to me now. Far be it from me to disagree too vociferously with Wallace Stegner, a writer I admire enormously. But some people are pretty natural short story writers, and some people are natural novelists. If you look at the careers of most writers who do both, I think you're going to find in most cases that the writer was better at one than the other.

Now, I've always liked Stegner's stories more than I liked his novels. That book of his, *The Collected Stories,* is a pretty spectacular book. William Trevor: I've liked his last two novels a lot. But I think he's the greatest short story writer alive, and one of the greatest ever. I think he's a better story writer. Alice Munro has written one book that has the word "novel" on it, but I would say it's a group of linked stories.

One exception: I think Richard Yates was a marvelous novelist and a wonderful short story writer. I really can't say that I think that he was better at one or the other. He's somebody that, unfortunately, is not being read much today. I really loved his work.

In 1986 you published an essay on the short fiction of Andre Dubus in which you argued that Dubus's sense of a short story's structure was intimately linked to how he handled characterization. How does a story's structure relate to character in your fiction?

Well, I think that the short story is peculiarly character-driven. And I think that the form of the story, whatever it happens to be, it should be what it is because in some way it helps you elucidate character. To go back to Dubus, there's a story of his—that essay, by the way, is drawn from my MA thesis, so I may be telling you something that's in the thesis and not in the essay—but there's a story of his called "Townies" that is divided into two sections. It's set in a small town in New England where there's a private college that has a lot of rich kids in it, and the opening section of that story begins with an elderly security guard walking across campus, I believe, early in the morning. He finds the body of a coed lying on a bridge, and she's been murdered. Beaten to death. That section ends with him, as I recall, kneeling over her and looking at her and thinking about what it's always felt like to be an outsider here. He's always looked at these girls and tried to imagine their lives, which are so different from his own.

Then there's a break, and we go backward in time. We're in the mind of another townie, a young man who has basically been living off these girls, ingratiating himself into their lives, and having them buy him things, and letting him stay in their places, listen to their music, and so forth. He turns out to be the one who has murdered that girl. And we end that story with him going back to his apartment or wherever he lives and waiting on the police that he knows will soon be coming to get him. But where we end it is prior to where we began. The story just stops there. So, it's a story that forms a circle, in a sense. And that starts seeming, you know, absolutely perfect when you think of the theme of the story, which has been what it feels like to be trapped in this town. To be a townie who, in some very real sense, can never be what these kids are, and who spends a lot of time thinking about it. So that's a story in which the whole structure, it seems to me, is something that just grows organically out of Dubus's conception of who those characters are. And I would like to think that when I'm really on the money in a story, the form of the story is what it is, again, because of who the characters are.

You got a MA in literary studies. As a writer, how has that training helped you?

I think it's very hard to be a really good writer without having some sense of the tradition that you're grounded in. In my classes at Fresno, I have a guy who's taken my classes a couple of times named Craig Bernthal. He's actually a Shakespeare scholar in our department. One thing I've noticed is that when Craig—who is already publishing his fiction now in good journals—would bring a draft of a story into the class, and it would have some problems, and you could tell him, "Well, this is a chance you're missing, and here's another one that could be exploited," or whatever, he would show back up two days later with this immaculate story where he had just played all those notes. And I found myself thinking, Now, he's really just started writing fiction, and he's about my age. Why is it happening so fast for him? Whereas somebody who's twenty or twenty-one years old, when you start pointing that stuff out, it takes a lot longer before they begin to get it. And I ended up thinking it's because of his literary training. He's able to intellectualize the concepts that you're talking about and just hit it, like that.

I wish everybody read more. I had a professor at Arkansas, a guy named Ben Kimpel, who's been dead now for fifteen or more years, who used to say, "Everybody ought to read everything." And he really meant it. It pained him enormously to think that there's going to be something out there that was really great that he might not be able to read before he died. To me, that was just the greatest example of what a literary person ought to be. And a writer ought to be a literary person.

Adultery is a common theme in your fiction. What is so compelling about this theme?

I think because the story seems to me to thrive on secrets. And so many of the short stories that I really love, that is the theme, including the story that I love more than any other. You can probably guess what it is: "The Lady with the Pet Dog." It seems to me that when you, in a basic technical sense, can put your characters in a short story in a situation in which the walls are closing in on them from the very beginning, in which they have very little space to operate, you put them under the kind of pressure that really will force them to define themselves before it's all said and done. If you look at adulterous relationships, they very quickly become two people against the world. And when they begin to unravel that's when it stops being two people against the world, a lot of the time. So, it's a perennial theme in the short story. I decided once upon a time that I've got to just start cataloging these stories and seeing how many great ones there are. I quickly ran out of catalog space in my own mind. But I think it has to do with the nature of secrecy and the kind of energy that places on a short story.

In your essay "Arms," there is an interesting passage in which you describe the racial fear that some whites feel in the Delta. They're afraid that, as you put it, the blacks will one day "take them over." Certainly, racial misconceptions abound in every corner of the United States. Does the racism you document in your fiction represent a particular form of a universal problem, or is there something unique about racism in the Delta?

I'm going to say yes to both. I think that the Delta is a very peculiar place for historical reasons. It's a place that's isolated. It's a harsh landscape. If nobody had ever done anything to it, if nobody had ever gone in there and burned the trees and cleared it, what you'd be looking at is a place where the only natural inhabitants are mosquitoes and snakes. That's it. Well, panthers and black bears. But, you know, dangerous creatures. It took a very tough and driven kind of person to come in there and battle those odds. What the early planters who came to the Delta figured out real quickly was that there was a hell of a lot of labor that had to be done here that needed manpower to do it. And so, initially, it was slaves. Later on, it was African-Americans living in something very close to slavery—another form of servitude. There were actually times when the planters in the Delta—and the biggest wave of this, if I recall correctly, was right around 1920—they were placing ads in newspapers in the hills in Mississippi trying to attract black people to the Delta, because there was a wave of migration out of the Delta. They began to get scared that they wouldn't have enough blacks there to do the labor.

God forbid they should have to do it themselves.

Absolutely. Or, that they should have to hire another person who, because of his skin color, would have to be treated like a man. They experimented with attempting to draw Italians. They even placed ads in train stations in Italy. At one point, the Italian embassy in the United States urged the Italian government to consider banning immigration to Mississippi because of the way people were going to be treated there. So, we're talking about a pretty hard history here.

The racial mix in many of the Delta counties has been pretty consistent for about 130 [or] 140 years. You'll find four blacks for every white person, or three blacks for every white person. A couple of the counties are about eighty or eighty-five percent African American. This in itself is unusual. Except for a couple of urban places like Washington, D.C., and perhaps Detroit, you don't find exactly that mix anywhere else in the country. So, it's a place where, for my money, you've got white people well aware that they've been outnumbered, and I think a lot of them have guilty consciences with, you know, pretty good reasons a lot of the time.

Racism exists everywhere. One thing I can say about white people and black people in the Delta is that in some very basic way they're not strange to one another. They know one another. There's not much that they can do that will surprise the other. And there are many places in America where you find whites who don't say the kinds of racist things that you'll hear said in the Delta, who will tell you that they don't have any racial prejudices at all. And that's true as long as they never have to encounter a person of another race. And, by and large, they manage to live their lives without ever doing that. So, it's a peculiar manifestation in the Delta, I think, of a problem that you find all over the world.

How different races perceive or read one another interests me greatly. That sense of the races "knowing" each other permeates a novel like Go Down, Moses. *As someone who hails from the Delta, how do you feel about Faulkner's presentation of race?*

The human interaction between African Americans and whites in Faulkner's work has almost always rung true for me. Which is to say that when I've read, for instance, the scenes between Dilsey and Jason in *The Sound and the Fury,* I feel like I've seen that before. Which is not to say that I think there's anything stereotyped about it, but just that it instantly, from the first time I ever read it, really rang true for me.

Now, would those portrayals be accurate to Oxford, Mississippi today? No. There've been changes. Nonetheless, my children were in public schools in Oxford in the fall. Oxford is one of the most liberal-minded towns in the south. It's a marvelous place. But my daughters noticed in the public schools that there was almost no interaction in school between African American children and white children. And that struck them as very odd, given the fact that they've lived most of their lives in Fresno County, which has a Hispanic majority. About forty-two percent. There are classes in Fresno County where you might have twenty or twenty-five different ethnic groups represented. There are problems there as well. But not this hard-and-fast line between two groups, which does still exist even in the best places in the south.

A character in one of your stories, "House of Health," says that Indianola is a town where everyone over twenty is married and their lives are "laid out in straight rows." Indeed, stratification in its many guises—social, economic, racial—is a common topic in your work. Yet you write of your characters with great compassion and sympathy. Is it fair to say you write not so much to articulate the despair or grief of your characters, but to show that such people can and do change? Is there a didactic impulse to any of your fiction?

There probably is. When I first started writing, I really looked down on my characters from a great height. I didn't like them. Finally I realized that if I was ever going to learn to love and accept myself, I was going to have to learn to love and accept the people I wrote about. And, in some ways, this is probably why I write. To find that acceptance in myself It's that old cliché, "To know all is to forgive all." I think that's a bit of an oversimplification, but I think the job of the artist is not only to introduce readers to people who are in some way different from themselves, and to open up those people's lives to the reader, but to introduce yourself, the writer, to somebody who is, in whatever way, different from you, and to accept those differences.

As your four published books show, you feel free to write from the point of view of the other. For example, you frequently write from a woman's point of view.

It seems to me to think otherwise, to say that you can only write about somebody whose experiences are essentially your own—I think that's not what art is about. It's the exact opposite of what it's about, or what I think it should be about. It's never bothered me to try to write from the point of view of a woman. I wrote a story that I haven't put in a book because I don't have enough stories to go with It. It was published in *Shenandoah* last year. It's a story set in Florence. Half of the story is from the point of view of an Italian woman who also happens to be a lesbian. I never felt that I couldn't write from the point of view of an Italian. I never felt that I couldn't write from the point of view of a lesbian. Now, I've got a lot of friends who are lesbians. I've got a couple of friends who are Italian. But, in a sense, that's beside the point. I felt like I knew that character and that I could handle it.

In the novel that I just finished, one of the main characters is an African American woman living in Mississippi in 1902. I write from her point of view, and I probably will be criticized for that when the book comes out. But, you know, the book is dedicated to just about my closest friend, a woman named Lillian Faderman, who is one of the preeminent lesbian critics in the country. And I talked to her before I ever wrote this book, and I said, "You know, I'm a little bit leery of this. I'm a little bit afraid to take this on." And her question was, Why? Of course you can do it." And I thought, Yeah, why not?

In a recent interview with Atlantic Unbound, *the on-line version of* The Atlantic Monthly, *poet and fiction writer Tess Gallagher said, "It's a great mystery to me how those writers who teach every year sustain their writing. I couldn't get to the deep water if I did it every year, all year. Sadly, universities don't help a writer protect the well they're drawing from." You're both a writer and a teacher of writing; does Gallagher's comment ring true for you, too?*

No. You can't look at one writer's circumstances and figure out much about what another writer needs to keep going. I've always felt like going into the classroom is a good thing, because I see a student doing something in a story and it doesn't work, and it makes me look at it and think, Why doesn't this work? Very often, it reminds me of something that I've tried, and I go back and look at that with a different eye and think, Now, does this work? Or, I have the experience of picking up a story—sometimes by a twenty-year-old person who's maybe writing a story for the first or second time—and it's just so damn good that it revs up my enthusiasm all over again for doing what I do. So, I've never looked at it as any kind of drawback.

Now, I know that for many writers it is. Some writers become so involved in their student's work that they can't get their own done. But, you know, I have to have a job, basically. And there's nothing I would rather do. I did screenwriting for a while and I made a fair amount of money doing that, but I could never say that I would rather do that. Teaching is much more exciting for me, and much more rewarding.

I think that it's very dangerous to go around and imagine a certain set of circumstances that have to exist before you can get your work done. Last spring, at Fresno, I was teaching three classes. My wife was teaching four. We've got two daughters who, in addition to our having to carry them to school and pick them up every day, were into piano lessons, went to a religion class at the Catholic church one day a week, and were into other activities at school. Well, on Tuesday, I would get home at 12: 15 after my class, and I had to pick them up at 1:00 and then I was running errands all afternoon. So, I had forty-five minutes in the middle of the day to write. I had no other time that day, so if I wanted to get anything done it had to be done then. And you know what I found at the end of the semester when I just started looking at what I had written when? My most productive day of the week was Tuesday. I did more work on Tuesday, and I did better work. I didn't have to rewrite much of what I did on Tuesday. On Monday, I had all day long. I carried them to school at 7: 15 and I picked them up at 3:00. I had all of those hours in between, and on the average I accomplished less than I did on Tuesday. So, if you want to do it, you'll do it.

You know where Faulkner wrote *As I Lay Dying?* He wrote it on the back of an overturned wheelbarrow in the basement of the power plant at the University of Mississippi in the middle of the night. He was down there taking care of the boiler. My recollection is he wrote it in a couple of months. So, if you want to do the work, you'll do the work, and if you don't want to do the work, you won't.

Do you think that's why so many people who graduate from MFA programs don't go on to publish and establish careers as writers?

Wasn't it Flannery O'Connor who said that the idea of being a writer appeals to a good many shiftless people? I may be paraphrasing. But if she didn't say it, she would have.

I don't know. I meet people like you, and you talk to them and pretty quickly you know that being a writer means almost everything to them. And then you meet a lot of people who say they want to be writers and you can't figure out why. You wonder if they really mean it. Very often the case is they want to see their name on a book jacket. But they don't get much joy out of sitting down and grappling with the words on the page. And because they don't, because they're not really intimately involved with it, or they don't need to do it, they don't do it.

And it's not for want of talent a lot of the time. A lot of people do have the talent. They have a way of looking at the world that would make it possible for them to write, but they don't have the need or the drive or the commitment. You know, a lot of people get married and they don't have the commitment, either. [laughs] And those marriages don't last.

The two personal essays I've read, "Preacher" and "Arms," are written in a voice and style not altogether different from your fiction. What prompted you to treat those subjects in nonfiction, rather than fiction?

I don't know. In the case of "Preacher," I was writing that essay right near the end of the O.J. Simpson trial. I really wanted to say, "Hey, this really happened." I wanted to drop that façade of fiction, even though the technique in the writing of that essay—with the exception of a kind of historical passage—is pretty much the same as you would use in a short story. There are details that, obviously, I could not have remembered real clearly. So, you end up using some scenic details just like you would in a short story. You can't truly remember word-for-word dialogue for forty years, so I would call that an example of creative nonfiction. And that's a term that's very much up in the air right now as to what that means or doesn't mean.

I went through a period in about '95 or '96 where I wrote a lot of essays. I actually thought I was working on a book of essays. And then, you know, I just couldn't think of any more to write. I went back to writing fiction. I finally wrote an essay about a month ago for a small magazine in Mississippi, *The Yalobusha Review,* because the Grisham writer writes an essay for it every year. That was the first nonfiction I had written, I think, in about two or three years. At a certain point, it quit coming to me.

I find the essay a wonderful genre. It's much freer, it seems to me, than the short story. It's a lot easier, emotionally, writing it. I don't think it places as much responsibility on you to develop character and conflict in the same way that a short story does. Even with what you referred to as the metafictional elements of my last book of stories, my conception of the short story is still pretty severe. There are certain things I expect a story to do. It may be that I'm just ignorant of the essay, but I think that it's a much more elastic term.

If you look at the people we think of as the great essayists—in this country, for me, that would be Gore Vidal and James Baldwin—and if you go back and look at the beginnings of the essay, like Montaigne, you find such an amazing diversity of approach. Vidal, sometimes his essays are almost narrative. At other times, in the guise of a book review, like the ones he writes for *The New York Review of Books,* are those book reviews or personal essays? It's difficult to say. Whereas, for me, a story is a story. I expect it to develop conflict and to dramatize the development of that conflict and to really deepen my conception of the characters. I'm much more open in terms of what I expect from an essay.

That mixing of genres has always intrigued me. Writers like Tim O'Brien or V.S. Naipaul intentionally blur the distinctions between fiction and autobiography.

In many literary cultures, there's no distinction made. If you pick up most literary journals in Poland, you'll find if there's any division at all, it'll be poetry and prose. They don't tell you whether the prose is a short story, or an essay, or a book review, for that matter, figuring that if it matters to you, you have the intelligence to figure it out, and if it doesn't matter to you, you just read it. That seems to me to be a pretty good state of affairs, but I'm not quite there yet.

You write frequently about music. Do you see any kind of relationship between music and writing?

The first thing I ever wanted to be was a musician. There was a television show that came out of El Dorado, Arkansas when I was a little kid called *The Big Ten,* which was a country music show on Saturday night. Most of the people who played on that show weren't professional musicians and they never became professional musicians. They were people like my family. They were dirt farmers, gas station attendants, or they worked in the oil fields. They were ordinary people. One thing that stuck with me about those folks—to the point that about three or four years ago I finally went back and wrote an essay about this television show and published it in *The Oxford American* and then *Reader's Digest* republished a short version of it a little over a year ago—was that these were people who had found a way to express themselves artistically. And it seemed to me, even as a child, that they had transcended some pretty mundane realities. So I began to look at music as a means of doing that.

Look at the realities that many of the early Delta bluesmen lived with. People like Charlie Patton and Robert Johnson. I think, from what I remember of his bio, Johnson never did that much manual labor. But I think I'm right in saying that Patton did. He worked on the plantation in Dockery, up in the northern part of Sunflower County. And yet these are people who made some of the most glorious music that has ever been made in this country. I think it came out of that urge to transcend a reality that was one that they really wanted or needed to escape from somehow. I think it's not hard to see how literature itself provides a means of escape.

When I was a kid, I read a lot of novels that, believe it or not, were actually set in Poland. Popular novels about the Second World War. Writers like Leon Uris. Books like *QB VII. Exodus. Mila 18. Mila* means "nice" in Polish. It's a street in Warsaw that was obliterated during the Second World War. On the one hand, the subject was unpleasant. On the other hand, it was something that took me away from my own reality and opened up a new world for me. And that's what music has always done for me as well. It's intimately connected with reading, for me. [It's] about the only thing I would perhaps like to have been other than a writer—and I'm not sure I would trade writing in for anything; in fact, I know I wouldn't.... But when you hear a great bluegrass guitarist, there's something magical about it.

In his 1985 essay "The Post-Modern Aura," Charles Newman writes, "I think it's fair to say that no serious fiction writer in America today can tell you whom he is writing for." Do you agree with Newman? Do you have a specific audience in mind when you write?

Always. The audience that I'm writing for is always my wife and my two daughters. Every word I write I'm aware that one day my children will read. And that's all I can say.

I know that, for instance, people in my home town read my work, and some of them don't read anybody else. I've had people tell me, "You're the only one I read." You know, like farmers or whatever. Some of the farmers down there are the *best* readers, but some of them aren't. They'll read anything that has to do with the town, so they read that. That's one audience.

In the age of the Internet, you certainly find out more about your audience. I've had people write to me and reveal that they've read all my books, so you know that those folks are out there. But I always want to know that when my kids read my work, when they're old enough to do that—and they've already read some of it, even though they're only eleven and twelve—that it will be the best I can do. So I always write with the awareness that those three people, for sure, are there. And I want them to believe what they see on the page.

2001

ABOUT THE INTERVIEWER: **Rob Davidson** is an Associate Professor of English at California State University, Chico. He is the author of *Field Observations*, a collection of short stories, and *The Master and the Dean: The Literary Criticism of Henry James and William Dean Howells*. He received an MFA in creative writing and a PhD in American literature from Purdue University, where he was the editor-in-chief of *Sycamore Review*.

About the Editors

Christopher Feliciano Arnold has written for *Playboy, Ecotone, Northwest Review,* and other magazines. His fiction has received awards from *The Atlantic Monthly* and The National Society of Arts and Letters, and special mention in the Pushcart Prize anthology.

Anthony Cook grew up in Cincinnati and now lives in Lafayette, Indiana. He has worked for the *Las Vegas Sun* and the *Cincinnati Post,* and now teaches writing at Purdue University.

Index of References to Authors and Works

Index

CPSIA information can be obtained at www.ICGtesting.com
Printed in the USA
237386LV00003B/9/P

9 781602 351783